The **Google Phone Pocket**Guide

Jason D. **O'Grady**

Ginormous knowledge, pocket-sized.

**Funding provided by
The Foundation for
Reading Area Community College**

**Peachpit
Press**

The Google Phone Pocket Guide
Jason D. O'Grady

Peachpit Press
1249 Eighth Street
Berkeley, CA 94710
510/524-2178
510/524-2221 (fax)

Find us on the Web at: www.peachpit.com
To report errors, please send a note to errata@peachpit.com.

Peachpit Press is a division of Pearson Education.

Executive editor: Clifford Colby
Editor: Kathy Simpson
Production editor: Cory Borman
Compositor: David Van Ness
Indexer: Valerie Haynes Perry
Cover design: Peachpit Press
Cover photography: courtesy of T-Mobile USA and Google Inc.
Interior design: Peachpit Press

ISBN-13:   978-0-321-62059-0
ISBN-10:   0-321-62059-3

9 8 7 6 5 4 3 2 1

Printed and bound in the United States of America

For Ginger and Elizabeth

About the Author

Jason O'Grady developed an affinity for Apple computers after using the original Lisa, and it turned into a bona-fide obsession when he got a 128k Mac in 1984. He started writing one of the first Web sites about Apple (O'Grady's PowerPage, www.powerpage.org) in 1995 and is considered to be one of the fathers of blogging. After winning a major legal battle with Apple in 2006, he set a precedent that gave independent journalists the same protections under the First Amendment as the mainstream media.

O'Grady is the author of *The Garmin nüvi Pocket Guide* (Peachpit Press) and *Corporations That Changed the World: Apple Inc.* (Greenwood Press), as well as a contributor to the eighth and ninth editions of the *Mac Bible* (Peachpit Press), and has contributed to numerous Mac publications over the years. He's currently blogging about Apple for ZDNet at The Apple Core (blogs.zdnet.com/Apple).

Acknowledgments

A heartfelt "Thank you" is in order to the people who helped me pull this book together.

Thanks to the awesome team at Peachpit Press: Cliff Colby, who kept the boat on course; my poor bug-hating editor, Kathy Simpson; production editor Cory Borman, who re-created all the status-bar icons; compositor David Van Ness; and indexer Valerie Haynes Perry.

Linda Tong from Android Product Marketing at Google, Inc., answered my late-night e-mails and provided the excellent icons that you see throughout the book. Special thanks to Jesse Friedman from Google Maps and Earth Marketing for keeping me oriented and to Kristen Resare from Waggener Edstrom Worldwide (for T-Mobile USA) for loaning me a G1.

A special shout-out to Pandora.com for providing the soundtrack for this book, especially my newly expanded Dub Reggae channel and several killer tracks, including Prince Far I's "Yes Yes Yes" (Errol Holt 12" Mix) and Dubblestandart's "Greetings from Evil Empire."

I'd be remiss if I didn't thank the staff at The Beach at Mandalay Bay, where I wrote Chapter 6, and also Red Bull Sugar Free, which "gave me wings" during many a late-night writing session.

Most of all, thanks for the loving support of my wife, Liz, and my daughter, Ginger, who fed me and kept me motivated during my nocturnal hours. Thanks, girls.

Contents

Introduction

When asked whether I'd be interested in writing a book about the Google phone, I immediately jumped at the offer. Although I've been a dyed-in-the-wool iPhone user since June 2007 (the day it came out), the Google phone has piqued my interest from the first day that I heard about it. Since the early rumors of a Google phone—or, more accurately, a Google *operating system*—I've been intrigued by the concept.

Most mobile phones these days (with the exception of Symbian-powered devices) run an operating system that the handset manufacturer made especially for it. Google bucked that trend. Instead, Google wrote a mobile operating system that was designed from the ground up for mobile phones and invited all comers. All handset vendors would be allowed to use the code on their devices. What a concept!

The Google mobile-phone operating system—which I'll refer to as *Android* in this book—is an intriguing piece of code. Anyone who uses Google's famous search portal (which is everyone, right?) knows that the company tends to deliver quality software, so naturally, expectations were quite high for its mobile-phone OS.

Anyone who uses a Google phone won't be disappointed. Android is a beautiful mix of fast-loading, intuitive applications that are perfect for novices and an open-source business model that will appeal to developers and tinkerers alike. It's got something for everyone. The included applications cover all the bases. Phone, contacts, calendar, e-mail, Web, messaging, camera—it's all there.

Probably the most powerful part of the Google phone is a virtual application store called the Android Market. The Market (as it's affectionately called) is a treasure trove of software that can be purchased, downloaded, and installed over the air directly from the phone. Although the application suite that comes with the phone offers all the basics, the Market offers thousands of applications for every business, market, and hobby imaginable.

I'm writing this book based on the G1 from T-Mobile, the first Android-based handset to be released. By the time you read the book, however, more than a dozen Android-powered phones will be on the market, and more will come after that. Heck, there's even talk of Android-powered tablets, netbooks, and notebooks down the road, so don't be surprised when you start seeing your favorite little robot popping up all over the place.

Now get ready to dive right in and start being productive with the Google phone and the Android operating system. If you have half as much fun using your Google phone as I had writing this book, you're in for a wild ride. Hang on; here we go!

Say Hello to the Google Phone

As you get started down the path to mastering the Google phone, some background information will help you form a good foundation of knowledge. In this chapter, I review some background on Google and Android, and explain how the Google phone came to be. Then I dive into the phone itself, the features, what comes in the box, and some tips and tricks about the user interface.

History and Background

One of the most compelling features of a Google phone is Google itself. The Silicon Valley search engine has grown into a search powerhouse that's used by just about everyone who uses the Internet. It's the default search engine in many Web browsers, which further contributes to its dominance. Google commands a substantial portion of search-engine market share in the United States—60 percent to more than 70 percent at this writing, depending on whom you believe.

About Google

Google was started by Larry Page and Sergey Brin while they were students at Stanford University and was incorporated in 1998. Google's initial public offering in 2004 raised an eye-popping $1.7 billion, making the company's value closer to $23 billion. Google stock (ticker symbol GOOG) shot as high as $700 per share in 2007 but at this writing (spring 2009) has settled down to around $370 per share, making the company worth around $117 billion. Not bad for a couple of Stanford students. The iconic Google home page is pictured in **Figure 1.1**.

 The name Google was derived from the word *googol*, which is 1 followed by 100 zeros, or 10^{100}.

Figure 1.1
The ubiquitous Google home page.

The company delivered results for north of 235 million searches per day in 2008. Having conquered search, it has since branched out into providing online (also called *cloud*) applications such as Google Docs and Google

Spreadsheets. Its free Web e-mail service, Gmail, was introduced in 2004 and has grown to more than 100 million accounts.

Most of these products are free, because Google subsidizes them with advertising, earning more than $21 billion in advertising revenue in 2008. Google's laserlike focus on specific keywords that *people are searching for* is highly desirable to advertisers and commands a premium price.

Google branched out into mobile search in 2000, delivering its fast, powerful search results to handheld devices such as smartphones. The company continues to refine and enhance its mobile-search product, and today, more than a third of Google searches in Japan are made on mobile devices.

About Android

In 2005, Google acquired a company called Android, with the intention of creating a carrier- and manufacturer-independent mobile operating system that would run on almost any type of hardware. The Google Android (**Figure 1.2**) is the logo and mascot of the operating system by the same name and has become synonymous with mobile devices. I'd pick the Google Android over the Linux penguin in a fight *any* day.

Figure 1.2
The Google Android, the mascot and logo of the mobile operating system by the same name.

Consumers got their first chance to use Android on October 22, 2008, when T-Mobile released the G1 phone in the United States. The G1 is frequently called the *Google phone* (hence, the name of this book) or the *gPhone* as a reference to Apple's iPhone. (Did I mention that there's a *Pocket Guide* for that device too? Check out *The iPhone Pocket Guide*, by Christopher Breen, also from Peachpit Press.)

Android is an open-source operating system, meaning that it's free to use and modify under the Apache and General Public License (GPL) licenses, which makes it very appealing to developers. Everyone from mobile phone carriers to handset manufacturers to individual developers can modify the operating system to accommodate their needs. No costly licensing fees or restrictions are associated with Android, as there are with other operating systems.

note When referring to a feature or function that's specific to the hardware, I'll discuss the T-Mobile G1 (or just G1). When referring to an aspect of the software, I'll discuss Android.

Expect Android to take off. Google is investing a lot of time and money in this operating system and is committed to making it a real competitor in the mobile-phone market. We're just starting to see the fruits of its labor. Developers are embracing Android because of its open-source roots and are signing up in droves to create applications (which I refer to as *apps* in this book) for the Android Market, which I cover in detail in Chapter 7.

Android has already been spotted in use on tablet and notebook computers, and because it's adaptable to many types of hardware platforms, I wouldn't be surprised to see it running on regular desktop computers in the future. Heck, you may have Android on your refrigerator door someday.

Open Handset Alliance

I'd be remiss if I didn't mention the Open Handset Alliance (**Figure 1.3**), a Google-led group established in 2007 to develop open standards for mobile devices. Its 34 member companies include most mobile-handset makers, application developers, carriers, and chipmakers.

Figure 1.3
The Open Handset Alliance's logo pretty much sums up the organization.

OHA distributes the Android Software Development Kit (SDK) and source code on its Web site at www.openhandsetalliance.com.

tip If you ever wonder whether a particular phone carrier is going to release an Android phone, you can check OHA's list of member companies. If the carrier is on the list, there's a good chance that it's working on releasing an Android-powered device.

Features

There are several reasons to purchase a Google phone, and the feature set is always expanding. In fact, one of the biggest advantages of owning a smartphone—any smartphone—is that you can customize it infinitely by adding your own software. If you're a developer, you can create apps yourself; the rest of us have to download them from the Android Market (see Chapter 7).

To begin, I'll review the core features that come with the Android operating system installed on a Google phone.

Mobile phone

The primary reason for buying a Google phone is the phone part. Right? Well, mostly yes, but it's not necessarily the main reason. Any way you look at it, the G1 from T-Mobile (**Figure 1.4**) is a very capable device.

Figure 1.4
The T-Mobile G1, the first Android device in the world.

COURTESY OF T-MOBILE USA, INC.

Under the hood, the G1 is a quad-band GSM/dual-band W-CDMA UMTS phone (see the nearby sidebar for translations). The phone itself has all the features you'd expect in a mobile phone and some other goodies too, such as voice dialing.

Alphabet Soup, Translated

Sorry for the alphabet soup; it comes with the territory. All those three- and four-character acronyms are short for different cell phone technologies. If you aren't a technical junkie, here's what they all stand for:

- **GSM:** Global System for Mobile Communication

- **CDMA:** Code Division Multiple Access

- **UMTS:** Universal Mobile Telecommunications System

The G1 has a pretty strong radio where I live, but as with any mobile phone, signal strength depends on the carrier's network (in this case, T-Mobile's) in your neighborhood.

tip You can check any U.S. address on the T-Mobile coverage map at www.t-mobile.com/coverage. All the U.S. mobile carriers offer similar tools on their Web sites.

E-mail

Another primary reason to buy a smartphone is to keep up with your ever-growing pile of unread e-mail. The G1 allows you to stay on top of your e-mail in style.

The included e-mail application seamlessly syncs messages from most POP3 (Post Office Protocol Version 3) and IMAP (Internet Message Access

Protocol) services, and displays graphics and photos inline courtesy of its rich HTML viewer. Also, the QWERTY keyboard on the G1 is a huge asset when you have to compose a long message.

tip If you use Gmail exclusively, you're in luck! Android includes a dedicated Gmail application in its default installation, If not, don't worry. Android handles all IMAP, POP3, and Web-based e-mail accounts without even breaking a sweat.

Gmail offers two-way synchronization of e-mail in real time (also known as *push*) so that you'll get notified when you receive new e-mails, even if you're in another application. Gmail even syncs draft e-mails, so you can begin writing a message on the Web and send it from the phone (and vice versa). Gmail for Android inherits many features from its desktop-based big brother, including labels, stars, and conversation view.

If you don't see the Gmail application on your phone, you can use the Web version (which is optimized for Android) at www.gmail.com or download it directly from the Market application. (See Chapter 7 for all the details on the Market.)

Messaging

Text and Multimedia Messaging Service (MMS) are extremely useful tools, and Android's Messaging application provides both in one app. Launch it to read and reply to messages you receive from your friends and colleagues. Received messages are threaded into a virtual conversation, making it easy to remember where you left off while bouncing among messages from different senders.

The Android Messaging application also makes it easy to flag, delete, and move groups of messages. The G1's full QWERTY keyboard pays dividends for people who text a lot.

Web browsing

The Web browser included with Android combines Google's legendary
search with a mobile version of its desktop Web browser, Chrome. Google
chose WebKit for its Android browser. WebKit, an application framework
that also powers Apple's Safari and Nokia's S60 browsers, is a full HTML
Web browser with a zoom function that allows you to zoom in and out
of any area of a Web page by tapping small magnifying-glass icons at the
bottom of the screen.

What's more, the Android Browser allows you to have multiple pages
open concurrently, and its bookmark and history interface is similar to
what you'd expect to find in a desktop Web browser. Simply click the
Menu button to access these features. To illustrate the fact that Google
thought of everything, the browser even includes *favicons*—the little
graphics that appear before the URL and before the <title> tag in
browser tabs.

Unfortunately, at this writing the Web browser bundled with Android
doesn't support Adobe Flash technology. This means that if you visit
a Web site that relies heavily on Flash, you may not get the full experience. Some sites use Flash for site navigation, making it virtually impossible to find your way around if you're using a non-Flash browser.

Contacts

A phone isn't a phone without someone to call. Google has chosen
an interesting method to sync contacts back and forth to the gPhone:
Google Contacts (www.google.com/contacts).

When you boot up your Google phone for the first time, you'll be asked
to log into your Google account. After you log in, your contacts are synced
automatically with the phone.

note If you're already a Gmail user, all your Gmail contacts will sync with your phone automatically. As you'd expect with a phone from Google, services from Google are baked into every aspect of the Android operating system.

The beauty of this system is that it's completely transparent and requires no user intervention whatsoever. You don't have to worry about discipline, USB cables, Bluetooth, or synchronization software; your contacts just sync in the background.

The down side is that if you're not a Google Contacts user, you'll have to import or enter your contacts to sync them to your phone. Fortunately, the process is Web-based (which definitely beats entering the contacts on the phone manually), and Google Contacts has excellent import tools.

The system supports importing contacts in the comma-separated values (CSV) file format from Microsoft Outlook, Outlook Express, Yahoo!, and Hotmail.

tip You can sync directly from Apple's Address Book by choosing Preferences > General (Figure 1.5). If you want to perform a one-time *import* from Address Book, use the freeware utility A to G (www.bborofka.com).

Figure 1.5
Apple's Address Book application syncs directly to Google Contacts.

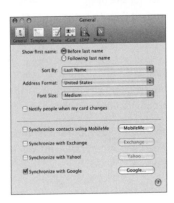

Calendar

Just like contacts, the Google phone's calendars sync with Google Calendar (www.google.com/calendar). Whatever information is in your Google Calendar gets synced with your phone automatically in real time, in the background.

gCalendar (as I like to call it) is loaded with features, including sharing, syncing with mobile phones and desktop software, reminders, invitations, and offline mode—not to mention that it's completely free. What a deal!

As with Google Contacts, if you're already a Calendar user, you're all set up. If you're not, you have a little work to do. Luckily, Calendar can easily import event information in iCal or CSV (Outlook) format. To get your calendars into Google, first export them from whatever software you're using now; then follow the import steps at the Google Calendar Web site.

Maps

One of the best features of the Google phone is Google Maps with Street View. When combined with your phone's built-in GPS (Global Positioning System) chip, Google Maps is one of the key advantages of owning the G1—or any other Android phone, for that matter.

Google set the bar for Web-based mapping services, and the mobile equivalent is as good as the Web version . . . if not better. I can almost hear you asking, "How can it be better?" The simple answer is MyLocation, which uses your mobile phone's GPS chip to pinpoint your location. Instead of entering your current location, you can simply ask the application for gas stations, ATMs, or sushi, and Google Maps will tell you where the sources closest to you are.

Google Maps provide map information, satellite imagery, and local business information. Street View provides virtual street-level exploration, courtesy of millions of pictures taken from a street-level perspective. The G1's built-in magnetometer (digital compass) orients Google Maps' Street View according to the position of the viewer and allows you to navigate 360 degrees simply by moving the phone around in your hand—an industry first.

YouTube

Google acquired YouTube in 2006 for $1.65 billion, and the child of this beautiful matrimonial union is a mobile YouTube application designed for the small screen and footprint of the Google phone. Although YouTube is great for watching videos of dogs skateboarding, it's also the default video player for most applications on the phone. YouTube has lots of business applications too, but I can't think of any right now.

YouTube for Android is loaded with features, including a catalog of millions of keyword-searchable videos that you can browse (most popular, most viewed, top rated, most recent, and most discussed). When you've found a video that you like, you can view its details, share it with a friend via e-mail, and even read the comments.

tip Although Android has a YouTube application, it's limited to viewing videos encoded in H.264/MPEG-4. This means that you can't play YouTube's voluminous library of Flash-encoded clips on the Google phone—only videos encoded in H.264.

Search

Google is the king of search, so it's pretty natural to expect excellent search on Android. You won't be disappointed. In addition to searching the Web, Google Search quickly finds news, images, and local businesses.

The Google phone takes search to the next level with Voice Search, which allows you to search for almost anything just by using your voice. Voice Search is available from the home screen and from the Web browser, making searching (especially while driving) easier and safer than ever.

The other killer app on the Google phone is MyLocation. As its name implies, this app allows you to search for things close to you based on your current location, thanks to the GPS chip in your phone. Although this feature may sound a little Orwellian, GPS can be extremely powerful when it's put to good use, which is one of the goals of this book.

When you're performing more traditional searches (with a keyboard), Google Suggest helps speed your typing by making suggestions on the fly. And because Google products are integrated, it's easy to check your Gmail or Calendar, or to access other Google products from within most Google apps. You can even customize the top menu bar.

Unboxing

Now that I've whetted your appetite with all these juicy features, you're ready to open the box and see what's inside. (Because you're reading this book, you've probably taken this step already, but just humor me, OK? And no, I don't blame you. I'm the type of person who usually can't make it out of the parking lot without ripping open the box of my new purchase.)

In this book, I focus on the T-Mobile G1 because it was the first Google phone to ship and is the only one on the market at this writing. Undoubtedly, dozens more Android handsets will be on the market by the time you read this book, so your box may come with slightly different contents, but the gist will be the same.

What's included

The packaging of the G1 is quite nice, being compact and organized, but I don't want to spend too much time on it, given how fast these things change. (If my publisher paid me by the word, that'd be a completely different story, but it doesn't, so I'll move on.)

Inside in the package, you'll find the following items:

- The phone itself
- T-Mobile SIM card
- Battery
- Mini USB wall charger
- USB-to-mini USB cable (for charging from a USB port)
- Mini USB stereo headphones with microphone
- 1 GB MicroSD card
- Nylon carrying case
- "Getting Started" guide
- Tips-and-tricks booklet

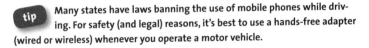 **tip** Many states have laws banning the use of mobile phones while driving. For safety (and legal) reasons, it's best to use a hands-free adapter (wired or wireless) whenever you operate a motor vehicle.

The headset that comes with the G1 has a mini USB connector because the G1 doesn't have a standard 3.5mm headset jack. The included earbuds are the round, hard kind and are nothing to write home about. If you want to use your own headphones or earbuds with the G1, you'll need to purchase a special adapter, which you can pick up for $6 to $16 on eBay and on Web sites such as www.G1depot.com.

A 1 GB MicroSD card is preinstalled in the G1, but you may have trouble finding it. The card is carefully hidden behind a tiny door on the left side of the phone, just to the left of the green Send key. You have to slide up the screen to access the tiny tab that opens the door. The G1 supports MicroSD cards up to 16 GB, which sell for about $40 apiece.

What's not included

Although everything that you need to get started is included in the box, you should consider purchasing a few extras:

- **Extra battery.** A second battery is practically a requirement for the G1. The included 1150 mAh (milliampere-hour) battery has been panned in reviews as woefully underpowered. Luckily, you can pick up extras online for around $10 each, so there's no excuse not to keep at least one on hand. If you're a power user, you can purchase extended-life batteries for the G1 that go as high as 2600 mAh for $55. The only problem is that higher-capacity batteries are larger and require a "humpback" rear panel (usually bundled with the battery) that makes the phone larger.

> **tip** It's a good idea to check the charge of stored rechargeable batteries periodically. Dormant batteries lose approximately 10 percent of their charge per month.

- **A real case.** The G1 case that comes from T-Mobile is of the sleeve variety and provides a minimum level of protection. Because you have to remove the phone to use it, though, this case is bound to get lost. Literally hundreds of mobile-phone cases are on the market, and they can be deeply personal. I'll leave you to your own devices to find one that suits your needs (and personality).

- **Screen cover/film.** If you tend to be rough on your gadgets (as I am), it's a good idea to invest in a screen film. This clear film sticks onto the screen of the phone, protecting it from scratches from keys, coins, and anything else that might be in your purse or pocket. Prices range from $3 to $15, and it's money well spent (if you don't like scratches, that is).

Controls and User Interface

To fully realize the potential of your Google phone, it's important to master the various hardware controls and interface elements that make all the magic happen. **Figure 1.6** gives you a close look at the controls and buttons on the T-Mobile G1 when it's oriented vertically (also called *portrait mode*).

Figure 1.6
The controls and user interface of the T-Mobile G1.
COURTESY OF T-MOBILE USA, INC.

Speaker/Status LED

Volume keys

Menu key

Camera key

Send key Trackball End key
Home key Back key

Sliding the keyboard out reveals the other major view of the T-Mobile G1: horizontal or *landscape mode* (**Figure 1.7**). Although the G1 is completely operable via its touchscreen with the keyboard concealed, many people prefer to use the hardware keyboard for texting and for composing e-mail.

Figure 1.7
The T-Mobile G1 with the keyboard exposed.
COURTESY OF T-MOBILE USA, INC.

Shift key
Search key
Enter key
USB port
ALT key
Space/Symbol key
SD card slot cover

The keyboard

The hardware QWERTY keyboard is a major feature of the G1, differentiating it from other Android phones. The vast majority of smartphone users probably would agree that a hardware keyboard is very desirable. Even casual e-mailers and pseudo-texters quickly realize the benefit of a hardware keyboard. Users who rely on their phones to send a lot of e-mail and/or text regularly already know the value of a QWERTY keyboard and may even have purchased the Google phone for this reason.

As keyboards go, the G1's version isn't stellar. For one thing, I have trouble finding keys on it without looking. For another thing, although I know that the G1 is a *phone* and isn't meant to replace a desktop computer's keyboard, I wish that the keys were a little taller, as they are on Palm smartphones. I also prefer keys that are a little rounder and more pebble-like—but hey, that's me.

note If you'd like to have less bulk and/or you're fine with using a virtual (onscreen) keyboard, you probably can find a thinner phone that runs Android.

Menu key

The Menu key (refer to Figure 1.6) is extremely useful in Android, and it's not available on other popular phones, such as the iPhone. Pressing it displays a small overlay on the bottom third of the screen, listing actions that are available in the current application. The Menu key is *contextual*, meaning that it presents different options depending on which app you're in. Usually, you can press it to find the various settings for a given application. (For more information on third-party applications, see Chapter 7.)

If you hold down the Menu key, the text labels below each option display their keyboard equivalents. Search becomes Menu+S, for example. People who use the keyboard a lot or simply are faster at typing sometimes prefer keyboard shortcuts to key presses.

Pressing the Menu key also unlocks the phone after the screen timeout interval (which you set by choosing Settings > Sound & Display) has elapsed.

Trackball

The trackball on the T-Mobile G1 (refer to Figure 1.6) is super-useful and an easy way to navigate the user interface. It's intuitive and requires little instruction, if any; simply roll it in the direction in which you want to move.

Use the trackball to scroll around the home screen to choose an application, or use it as a controller in any of the many games that are available in Android Market. It also doubles as a button. After you've found the application that you're looking for, you can click the trackball in to launch the application. In case you're wondering, this trackball is the same one that Research In Motion (RIM) uses in many of its BlackBerry devices.

Home key

The Home key (refer to Figure 1.6) is equally intuitive. Pressing it takes you . . . well, home. It's a nice escape hatch from the depths of your Google phone and a simple way to find your way back after an adventure through its various settings, menus, and applications.

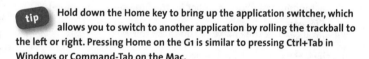 **tip**   Hold down the Home key to bring up the application switcher, which allows you to switch to another application by rolling the trackball to the left or right. Pressing Home on the G1 is similar to pressing Ctrl+Tab in Windows or Command-Tab on the Mac.

Back key

Another unique feature of the T-Mobile G1—and another one that's not available on the iPhone—is the Back key (refer to Figure 1.6). As you'd expect, it takes you back to the last screen that you viewed. In fact, the Back key operates exactly like the Back button in the Web browser that you've come to know and love.

The Back key also functions like the Escape (or Esc) key on a standard computer keyboard, in that it dismisses dialog boxes and the menu interface. If you want to get out of where you are but don't necessarily want to go home, the Back key is for you.

Send and End keys

The Send (green) and End (red) keys (refer to Figure 1.6) are going to be familiar to anyone who's ever used a mobile phone. Press Send to place a call after dialing a number, and press End to hang up on a call, disconnecting the other party.

On the G1, however, the venerable green and red keys do a lot more. You can use the Send key to do the following things:

- Bring up the Voice Dialer (by pressing and holding the key)
- Open the recent call log
- Call a contact when a name or number is highlighted onscreen
- Add another call to the current call
- Display the current call onscreen if you're in another application
- Call the highlighted phone number (in the browser, for example)

Likewise, you can use the End key to do these things:

- Lock the screen and put the phone in sleep mode
- Power off the phone (by pressing and holding the key)
- Toggle silent mode on or off

The End key is the perfect way to end Chapter 1. Now that you've had a look at the background, features, and general controls of the Google phone, it's time to see how to set up the phone for the first time and how to use and understand statuses, notifications, and applications. You do all that in Chapter 2.

Google Phone Basics

You saw in Chapter 1 that there's a lot going on under the Google phone's hood and that it's packed with features. Now it's time to dive into some of the basics of owning and using an Android-powered phone—things that will soon become second nature but take a little time to master.

This chapter builds on that strong foundation that you started in Chapter 1. I review the finer points of your gPhone's battery and memory card, and give you an in-depth look at the home screen and application list.

Here we go!

Setting Up the Phone

On your maiden boot of a Google phone, the phone steps you through several screens that are very important in the overall scheme of things. These screens help you set up your Google account, which will be the primary account on the phone. When you enter your Google account information, the gPhone uses that information to sync your e-mail, contacts, and calendar events from the cloud to your phone. (Flip back to Chapter 1 if you need a refresher on the cloud.)

After turning on the phone, you'll be greeted by the Android mascot. Then an informational screen (**Figure 2.1**) reminds you that you need a Google account to continue.

Figure 2.1
Setup introduction screen.

note Any Google login will work here. If you've got a Gmail, Google Docs, or other Google password, you can use it to register your phone. If you have more than one Google account, link your phone to the account you use most.

tip Usually, a Gmail account works best because it already has your e-mail contacts in it.

Signing in

The next screen asks you to sign in with your existing Google account or create a new one (**Figure 2.2**).

Figure 2.2
In this screen, you can either create or sign in with an existing Google account.

Signing in is easy if you already have a Google account. Just tap the
Sign In button shown in Figure 2.2. Then, in the next screen (**Figure 2.3**),
enter your Google user name (or your Gmail address) followed by the
matching password, and tap the Sign in button in the bottom-right
corner of the screen. When you tap Sign In, you're agreeing to Google's
terms and privacy policies, which is required.

Figure 2.3
*Signing in with
your existing
Google account
also requires
accepting
Google's terms
and policies. You
can't do much
about that.*

tip   In addition to tapping the screen, you usually have three ways to
acknowledge the default button or selected option on the screen:
Click the trackball, press the Return key on the keyboard, or press the Send key
on the bottom of the phone. Some people find it quicker to press or click than to
tap. As far as I'm concerned, more choices are always better.

Setting up your account

After you've promised your life away to Google, you're on your way to
Google bliss! (Actually, it's not that exciting; I take it back.)

In the next screen (**Figure 2.4**), you're warned that it could take an entire
5 *minutes* to set up your account. Time to mow the lawn! (In fact, my
account took all of 90 seconds to sync over the 3G T-Mobile network in
my neighborhood.) Account setup is a pretty quick and painless process.

Figure 2.4
*After you enter
your login
credentials, your
gPhone account
is created in less
than 5 minutes.*

Syncing your account info

When your basic account information has downloaded from Google,
you're off to the races. Simply tap the Finish Setup button (**Figure 2.5**,
on the next page), and you can start using your phone right away.
Downloading your account information is quick and painless because
the phone doesn't initially download the thousands of e-mails, contacts,
and calendar events you may have stored in the Google cloud—just
your basic account info. After your account info is synced, your contacts,
calendar events, and e-mail begin downloading to your phone in the
background.

Figure 2.5
Success! Your gPhone is ready for a test drive.

When the syncing icon disappears from the status bar at the top of the screen, the download is complete. (I cover the status bar in more detail later in this chapter.)

note   Whenever you receive a new message or alert, an icon appears in the status bar. For more info on these icons, see "Getting to Know Notifications" later in this chapter.

Getting online

Now that your phone is set up and accessing the Internet, it's time to put down the book for a while and have some fun. I encourage you to take 30 minutes to an hour to explore the phone's interface and applications.

You'll get the hang of it really quickly. If you know how to use the Internet, you already know how to use the Google phone.

On the home screen (**Figure 2.6**), tap the Browser application to surf (press the Menu key for more options), or tap Dialer to make a call. For a fun diversion, tap the gray arrow at the bottom of the screen to see a list of all of the applications installed on your phone. I give you a detailed look at all these elements in "Touring the Home Screen" later in this chapter.

Figure 2.6
*The Android
home screen.*
COURTESY OF T-MOBILE USA, INC.

Enjoy yourself—but come back to the book soon! I've got important things to say about batteries and expansion cards that you'll want to know about.

Charging and Conserving the Battery

The T-Mobile G1 comes with a rechargeable Lithium-ion battery that the manufacturer claims will allow you to talk for 5 hours or keep the phone on standby for 130 hours. Unfortunately, the reality is closer to about half that.

In fact, the G1's battery (shown installed in **Figure 2.7** and removed in **Figure 2.8**) is probably its worst feature. The included 1150 mAh (short for *milliampere-hour*) battery pack is simply too underpowered to handle a full day's smartphone use. Luckily, higher-capacity batteries are available from third parties (more on that topic in the next section), and technology advances very rapidly. The next round of Android-powered phones undoubtedly will focus on improving overall battery life.

The Subscriber Identity Module (SIM) card identifies a mobile customer and his provider. A SIM card must be inserted into the user's mobile phone before the phone can be used.

Figure 2.7
The rear of the T-Mobile G1 with the battery and SIM card installed.

note If you're a heavy user, pay attention to the mAh of the included battery and any extras you're considering buying. Although a higher mAh will give you a longer run time, sometimes it comes at the expense of bulk. Some high-cap batteries (which go as high as 2600 mAh at this writing) protrude from the rear of the phone, making your phone larger and heavier.

Figure 2.8
The battery and SIM card removed for a closer look.

First charge

When you first start your Google phone, the included battery can have anything from zero to a partial charge. Assuming that you don't have to run out the door *right now* with it or anything, I recommend connecting your phone to the wall charger to give it a good solid charge.

According to the manual, you should charge the gPhone's battery the first time for 12 hours, although overnight usually is perfect thereafter. I don't know about you, but there's almost *zero* chance that I'll put down a new gadget long enough to charge it fully. It's fun to find a comfy chair next to an outlet, plug in the G1, and explore around while it charges the first time.

Like most Android-powered phones, the G1 comes with a Lithium-ion (abbreviated *Li-ion*) battery. This battery doesn't suffer from the "memory effect," in that you don't have to drain it completely before recharging it. I still try to fully charge my G1's battery whenever possible, but this practice is mostly habit (and partly superstition?) and isn't necessary.

You have two ways to charge most Google phones:

- **Charger cable.** The charger cable (**Figure 2.9**) came in the box with your phone. You've probably charged devices with a cable like this since you were 5 years old, so I'll let you figure that one out yourself. On the G1, the charging port is located on the bottom edge of the phone under the trackball. To get access to it, you need to flip down a little door.

Figure 2.9
*The standard
G1 charger cable,
which you'll
probably be using
a lot.*

- **USB port.** The alternative is to plug your phone into an available USB port on a computer, using the included USB cable. This method is a boon if you travel with a notebook computer because you can charge you phone simply by connecting it to your notebook via USB.

note Be careful here: The host computer must be awake, not in sleep or hibernate mode, to charge via USB. Most computers turn off their USB ports while sleeping, which will prevent your phone from charging.

Charging strategy

Your charging schedule depends on how you use your Google phone. If you're a casual user who places and receives fewer than 10 calls per day and uses the phone's Internet features only periodically, I recommend that you charge your phone each night while you sleep. Although the phone may not *need* a charge at the end of each day, charging nightly is a hedge against the chance that you'll have an unexpectedly busy day tomorrow and your phone will run out of juice just when you need it most.

If you're a heavy user of features such as 3G and Wi-Fi, you can literally watch the battery meter trickle down as you use the phone, and you need to plan accordingly. Heavy users will have a tough time making it through a standard business day on a charged 1150 mAh battery, like the one included with the G1. If this sounds like you, you'll want to read the upcoming sections on extra batteries and conservation methods.

Battery life

Battery life depends on the battery that comes with your phone. This book discusses the T-Mobile G1's 1150 mAh battery; as the saying goes, your mileage may vary.

The folks at T-Mobile claim that the G1 battery will allow you to talk for 5 hours or keep the phone in standby mode for 130 hours. Unfortunately, most users experience much less actual run time—something like *half* as much. Again, battery consumption depends on several factors:

- **Phone activity.** The first factor is how often the phone is on and running—that is, not in sleep/hibernate mode.

- **Screen brightness and timeout settings.** It takes a lot of power to light up the large, complex screens that come with smartphones. Keeping the phone on longer than necessary, and keeping the screen brighter than necessary, will consume more battery power. It's common sense.

- **Radio use.** The *radios*—transmitters and receivers—you use are major consumers of battery power, and a Google phone has lots of radios. The G1 includes radios for GSM (phone), Edge, 3G, Wi-Fi, Global Positioning System (GPS), and Bluetooth.

For tips on battery conservation, read on.

Conservation techniques

High-tech smartphones with lots of power-hungry radios can chew through a charged battery pack before the clock strikes noon if you're not careful. These battery management and conservation techniques can take you a long way:

- **Turn off features that you don't use.** If you don't use Wi-Fi, GPS, and 3G, turn them off in Settings. You'll get much longer battery life by using 2G, which is tolerable for light surfing and e-mail.

- **Keep the screen at the lowest brightness that you can tolerate.** To adjust the brightness, tap Settings > Sound & Display, and scroll down to the bottom of the list. The same goes for the screen timeout setting: Keep it at 1 minute, and turn the screen off when you're not using it by pressing the End key.

- **Disable autosync if you don't need real-time e-mail.** Tap Settings > Data Synchronization to change this setting. Turning off autosync stops your phone from constantly accessing the Google servers to download e-mails, calendar events, and contacts. Although you choose which of the three items to sync in Settings, if you sync one, you might as well sync them all.

- **Use shortcuts for frequently used applications.** Using shortcuts (tap Settings > Applications > Quick Launch) saves screen taps and scrolls, and shortens the amount of time that the screen is on.

- **Install new firmware updates on your phone shortly after they're released.** Firmware updates almost always improve battery life in addition to adding features and fixing bugs. To check whether you're due for a system update, tap Settings > About Phone > Status > System Updates.

tip An application called Locale, which is available in the Android Market, can manage almost every aspect of a Google phone dynamically, including neat things such as automatically switching to your home Wi-Fi network when it's in range and turning off 3G and GPS. Locale is an amazing app, and the best part is that it's free. For details, see the Locale Web site (www. twofortyfouram.com). I cover applications and the Android Market in Chapter 7.

Extra batteries

As I mention (several times) earlier in this chapter, smartphones eat through batteries like they're going out of style. Even a moderate user will need a backup battery before too long, so a backup is practically a requirement.

Replacement batteries (**Figure 2.10**) are relatively cheap, at less than $10 for a 1200 mAh pack, which makes purchasing them a no-brainer. Pick up one or two on eBay, and keep one in your car at all times.

Figure 2.10
You can purchase third-party 1200 mAh batteries on eBay for less than $10.

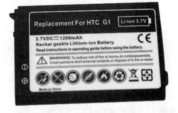

note Charge and rotate the batteries often. Batteries of this type lose about 10 percent of their charge per month and discharge completely before you know it.

If you want more power, you can purchase a battery as high as 2600 mAh for around $50 on the aftermarket. This type of battery effectively doubles your Google phone's run time. The problem is that large batteries like the 2600 mAh monster include a replacement rear cover to cover the extra bulge. Think in terms of a trade-off: You can have longer run time if you're willing to add some size and weight in exchange.

Managing the Memory Card

A great feature of the G1 and of future Android phones is the included expansion-card slot, which allows you an infinite amount of expansion beyond the paltry 57 MB of internal memory that's available on the G1. Expansion cards have unlimited uses and capacity; you can add as many cards as you need.

The expansion-card slot is a key feature that's not available in the Google phone's largest competitor: the iPhone. You can mention this handy gPhone feature next time someone's getting on his iPhone soapbox.

MicroSDHC cards

The expansion-card slot on the G1 accepts MicroSDHC (Micro Secure Digital High Capacity) cards, which are even smaller than the SD cards used in many digital cameras. MicroSDHC memory cards are just a hair over half an inch on their longest side and are easy to lose, so keep them in a safe place.

 Google refers to these cards simply as SD cards in some Android menus, but don't let that term throw you.

The largest-capacity MicroSDHC card currently supported in the G1 is 16 GB, which is more than you'll probably need. The 1 GB card that comes with the G1 is nice but isn't going to last too long. I recommend that casual users purchase an 8 GB MicroSDHC card (around $15 at this writing) and that power users buck up for the larger 16 GB card, which runs around $45.

Due to Moore's Law (which I define in the following tip) and the dynamics of book publishing, there's a good chance that 32 GB, 64 GB, or even 128 GB MicroSDHC expansion cards could be available by the time you read this book. Before you buy one, make sure that the Android operating system you're running supports the larger card. A 32 GB card is a waste if the firmware you're running recognizes only 16 GB of it. Check your firmware by tapping Settings > About Phone > Status and scrolling down to the build number.

> **tip** Moore's Law describes a trend in the history of computing hardware in which the number of transistors on an integrated circuit doubles approximately every 2 years.

MicroSDHC slot

Getting at the card itself can be challenging. In fact, if you haven't read ahead, take a minute and try to locate the memory-card slot. Go ahead; I'll wait.

Could you find it? (Be honest!) Don't worry if you couldn't; most people can't find the slot on the T-Mobile G1. That's because it's hidden behind a tiny door on the left side of the handset, next to the green Send key (**Figure 2.11**). A tiny release tab appears just inside the front edge of the lip when you slide the screen to the open position.

Figure 2.11
The well-hidden expansion-card slot on the left side of the G1.

This slot is also a challenge to open if you have large mitts, but a fingernail is usually enough to pop the door open. After you get the door open, insert the card as shown in **Figure 2.12**, with the gold contacts down and the wider side (with the notch) to the right. Luckily, MicroSDHC cards are keyed so that you can't insert them the wrong way.

Figure 2.12
A MicroSDHD card shown in its correct orientation for insertion into the G1.

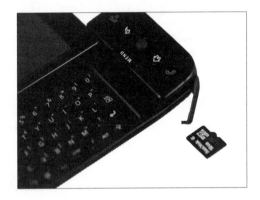

When you have the card inserted properly, you'll hear a click. Close the door, and you're ready to use the additional storage capacity for apps, music, movies, or whatever you want. When you run out of room, you can always get another card. Take that, iPhone!

After a card is installed, you can unmount it and view available storage by tapping Settings > SD Card & Phone Storage (**Figure 2.13**).

Figure 2.13
You can view the available space on your SD card in the SD Card settings screen.

Touring the Home Screen

Welcome home. I've been expecting you.

The Android home screen (**Figure 2.14**) is like your desk: It's where you use and organize your applications in a way that's most effective for you.

Figure 2.14
The Android home screen is where you end up when you press the white Home key on the front of the phone.
COURTESY OF T-MOBILE USA, INC.

— Status bar
— Dialer
— Contacts
— Browser
— Maps
— Application drawer

Because you go to the home screen after pressing the convenient Home key, you should dedicate it to shortcuts for your most frequently used applications. Out of the box, Google puts the four most commonly used applications on the home screen: Dialer, Contacts, Browser, and Maps. (Actually, it includes five if you count the big analog clock staring at you front and center.) T-Mobile also adds an application called myFaves to the home screen of the G1.

Customizing your home screen

The best feature of the home screen is that it's completely customizable. Tap and hold an icon, and a slight vibe tells you that now you can move that application. Tap and hold an empty space to add any application, shortcut, or widget to a home screen. My Android home screen is very dynamic, as I continually shuffle and shift apps between pages.

> **tip** You can swipe left and right on the home screen to reveal two additional home screens (for a total of three). These secondary home screens are great for storing shortcuts for apps that you use less frequently or that don't quite make the cut to the big leagues.

Removing application icons

When you want to remove an app's icon from the home screen (and this *will* happen), simply tap and hold it. You'll notice that the gray triangle on the application drawer turns into a trash can. (I cover this drawer at the end of the chapter.) Simply drag the application icon to the trash can to remove that icon from your home screen. The icon and the trash can glow red when they touch, confirming the deletion (**Figure 2.15**).

Figure 2.15
Removing an application icon from the home screen.

> **note** This procedure doesn't delete the application itself from your phone—just the shortcut or alias to the app. For details on deleting the app, see the next section.

Uninstalling and managing apps

To permanently remove (*uninstall,* in Android parlance) an application that you've downloaded, simply follow these steps:

1. Launch Android Market (see Chapter 7).

2. Click the Menu button.

3. Tap My Downloads.

4. Scroll to the app that you want to uninstall.

5. Tap the Uninstall button.

You can't delete some of Android's core applications—such as Gmail (**Figure 2.16**), Contacts, and Calendar—but you can manage any application by tapping Settings > Applications > Manage Applications and then tapping the app's name. This method can be useful if you need to clear data or manage space within the Gmail application, for example.

Figure 2.16
Managing a core application—in this case, Gmail.

Checking the Status Bar

Another defining feature of Android is its ingenious status bar permanently affixed at the top of the screen (**Figure 2.17**). Think of the status bar as being a clearinghouse for all the alerts, messages, alarms, and other notifications you could possibly receive on a mobile device . . . and then some.

Phone reception bars   Battery level
Network indicator | | Time display

Figure 2.17
*A standard
Android status
bar.*

 tip   Tap the status bar to briefly display the date on the left side.

The Android status bar, like memory expansion and the removable battery, is another key feature that's not available in the iPhone. (I'm not trying to start any sort of class warfare or anything, but there are lots of benefits to having a gPhone instead of an iPhone, which I'll continue to point out in this book.)

The status bar is rather small, so icons and symbols can be hard to discern, especially some of the less common ones. (I provide a chart of common notification icons in the following section.) You can pull down the status bar by tapping it and dragging down without lifting your finger. This drag reveals a resizable (up to full-screen) display of all your current status notifications and more information about each one, such as your number of unread e-mails. Tapping any of these extended notifications takes you directly to the application that produced it so that you can listen to the voice mail or read the text message, for example.

Equally handy is the large Clear Notifications button in the top-right corner of the screen (**Figure 2.18**). It's amazing how many notifications Android can generate, especially if you receive a lot of e-mail and text messages, and if you're on a social network such as Twitter, Facebook, or MySpace, be prepared to be inundated by notifications. The Clear Notifications button will come in handy plenty of times. (I cover notifications in detail in the next section.)

Figure 2.18
The Clear Notifications button can come in handy when the little devils get out of control.

The status bar is available to every application that you download, so be prepared to see all kinds of new icons pop up in it from time to time. Luckily, almost every application allows you to choose how you receive its notifications. If your status bar is getting cluttered with alerts, like the one in **Figure 2.19**, press the Menu button when you're in the offending application; then find the setting to change how it notifies you. Good applications offer many notification options; bad ones don't (and sometimes make it hard to find the notification settings).

Figure 2.19
Here's a good example of a bunch of alert notifications clogging the status bar.

Getting to Know Notifications

Notifications are integral parts of the Google-phone ecosystem. They're used generously by the operating system and by most third-party applications too. Getting up to speed on the gPhone's notification icons will make you much more efficient in using your phone, because you'll be able to identify those icons on the go.

Figure 2.20 shows a chart of the most common notification icons and their meanings. Most of these icons are self-explanatory; others, not so much.

Figure 2.20
Most of the standard notification icons you'll find in the status bar.

Icon	Description	Icon	Description
	New e-mail message		Ringer is off (silent mode)
	New text or picture message		Ringer on vibrate only
	Problem with text or picture message delivery		Phone is on mute
	New instant message		GPS is on and is working
	New voicemail		Uploading / downloading
	Upcoming event		Content downloaded
	Alarm is set		GSM signal, roaming, no signal
	Song is playing		GPRS service connected, data flowing
	Data is syncing		EDGE service connected, data flowing
	SD card is full		3G service connected, data flowing
	More (undisplayed) notifications		Wi-Fi service connected, network available
	Call in progress		Battery charge indicators (full, half-full, low, very low)
	Missed call		Battery is charging
	Call on hold		Wireless services are off
	Call forwarding is on		Bluetooth is on, Bluetooth device connected
	Speakerphone is on		No SIM card

Working with the Application Drawer

The home screen (refer to "Touring the Home Screen" earlier in this chapter) is where you store icons for frequently used apps, shortcuts, and widgets. Tapping the application drawer (refer to Figure 2.14) opens the drawer to reveal a list of all the applications currently installed on your Google phone (**Figure 2.21**).

Figure 2.21
The application drawer displays all the apps on your phone.

The application drawer is arguably the most exciting aspect of the Google phone because it gives you unlimited freedom to customize your phone with applications that suit your specific needs.

Applications are sorted alphabetically. You can scroll through them vertically with upward or downward flicks anywhere inside the open drawer. You can launch an app from the drawer by tapping it, clicking the trackball, or pressing the Return or Send key on the keyboard.

I discuss applications in much more detail in Chapter 7, which covers the Android Market. In the meantime, I want to give you a closer look at some of Android's core features such as the phone, contacts, and calendar, which I do in Chapter 3.

3

Phone, Contacts, and Calendar

Whereas Chapters 1 and 2 are designed to give you some background and get you up and running quickly with your Google phone, this chapter starts a more hands-on section of the book. It's time to turn your attention to productivity, and specifically to three of the core applications on the gPhone: the phone itself and the Contacts and Calendar features.

In this chapter, I explore these tools, which are absolutely essential to communications and productivity. I start with the basics and then show you a few tips that will improve your productivity and hone your skills.

Phone

The phone part of a smartphone is its most important feature. (I almost wrote that it's *arguably* the most important feature, but there's really no argument to be made.) Any mobile phone needs to function well as a phone first and foremost. If your new smartphone doesn't work well as a phone, it's basically useless.

Mobile phones (or *handys*, as they're called in the United Kingdom) have shrunk the world to the size of a thimble, allowing us to communicate more easily than we've ever been able to in the past. They've also saved countless lives by enabling people in distress to call for help. The safety implications alone underscore the importance of having a mobile phone—more important, one that's reliable and can make emergency calls easily. A phone with all the features in the world doesn't help you if it's lousy at making phone calls.

Luckily, the Android operating system makes a heck of a nice phone. The Google phone has all the features that you'd expect in a modern mobile phone—and then some. Also, because Google is committed to continuing to improve it, it's only going to get better.

note With any mobile phone, your coverage is only as good as your provider's infrastructure (number of towers and roaming agreements) *in your neighborhood*. Before buying any mobile phone, find a friend who has a phone on that carrier's network, and test that phone vigorously at your house and office before you sign up for a contract. Most carriers offer a limited return policy—usually within 7 to 30 days after purchase, but the duration varies from state to state.

The Android Dialer application (**Figure 3.1**) is very sleek and simply designed. Four tabs across the top give you easy access to all its functions:

- **Dialer.** Allows you to tap the screen to dial a number. (Many people find it easier to tap the number on the keyboard, however.)

- **Call Log.** Displays a list of your recent inbound and outbound calls. Pressing the Menu key gives you the option to clear the call log.

- **Contacts.** Contains all the names and phone numbers stored on your phone. I discuss contacts in detail in the next major section of this chapter.

- **Favorites.** Allows you to store your frequently dialed numbers (family members, friends, the office) in one convenient location. Tapping the star icon for any contact adds that person to your favorites list.

Figure 3.1
The ubiquitous Android Dialer application.

Incoming and outgoing calls

Making a call on the Google phone couldn't be much easier:

1. Dial a number.

   If you have a phone with a keyboard, the fastest way is to simply slide the keyboard out and start typing numbers on it. Android assumes that you want to dial a phone number and immediately launches the Dialer application. Even if you don't have a slider phone, pressing numbers on the keyboard launches the Dialer application.

2. Press the green Send key to initiate the phone call (**Figure 3.2**).

Figure 3.2
Dialing a phone number.

3. When the phone is dialing, press the Menu key to bring up a series of call options (**Figure 3.3**).

You'll find that the Hold and Mute buttons come in handy for any number of reasons, including sparing the recipient of your call the shriek of a siren passing in the street. Other call options—such as Speaker and Merge Calls—are covered later in this chapter.

Figure 3.3
Pressing the Menu key during a call brings up several options.

4. Simply listen for the other party and start talking when you hear him.

Because my daughter has been doing this since around age 1, I'm not going to go into too much detail on this step.

If someone is calling you, her phone number is displayed on your screen. If she's in your contacts database, her name also appears here. To answer, press Send.

As with most other mobile phones on the market, pressing the red End key—you guessed it—ends the phone call. No surprises there.

Speakerphone

The speakerphone is an excellent feature of the Google phone. To access it, press the Menu key during any phone call to display the call-options screen (refer to Figure 3.3) and then tap Speaker. You'll hear your caller through the phone's larger speaker, and he'll hear you through the built-in microphone.

Speaker is an excellent feature to use for long calls. It also comes in handy when someone's giving you instructions on how to upgrade your computer, for example, when you need both hands free for delicate work or have to crawl under a desk.

Although this feature is very handy, use it with discretion. Do *you* like being put on speakerphone? Most people don't, so ask for permission first. Also use this feature sparingly. Being underneath a car that you're trying to repair is a legitimate reason to put someone on speakerphone, but tapping Speaker all the time because you're too lazy to hold the phone isn't.

Hang Up and Drive

Using a speakerphone while driving is popular because it allows you to keep both hands on the wheel. Many U.S. states have passed laws making it illegal to operate a mobile phone while operating a motor vehicle, and speakerphones fall into a gray area. Driving while talking over a speakerphone technically is allowed in most states, but the phone has to be sitting on the seat or in a cup holder—*not* in your hand. As soon as you touch it to dial or hang up, you may be breaking the law.

I don't recommend using the Speaker feature while driving because it's still a distraction. Instead, pick up a good Bluetooth headset (which I cover in Chapter 4).

Conference calls

Another powerful and somewhat underused feature of most mobile phones these days is the conference call. Conference calls are a super-handy way to shore up plans with multiple people, and they're dead simple to set up on the gPhone, so there's really no excuse not to learn how to do it. Here's how:

1. When you have one person on the phone, press the Menu key to reveal the call-options screen (refer to Figure 3.3).

2. Tap Add Call, and dial the next party.

3. When the second party is on the line, press the Menu key again to reopen the call-options screen.

4. Tap Merge Calls.

Congratulations—you've made your first conference call on the gPhone. I told you that it would be easy!

note There's no physical limit on the number of people you can have on a conference call on Android—just a practical limit. I think that managing more than five people on a call gets a little hard, but hey, that's me.

Call waiting

Just like your landline phone at home (if you still have one, that is), the Google phone has call waiting built in. When you're on one phone call and another call comes in, you should see a screen that looks like **Figure 3.4**, displaying the caller's number. Most mobile carriers in the United States include Caller ID in their plans, and Android also displays the incoming phone number if it's not blocked or private. If the caller is in your contacts database, the gPhone also displays that person's name and any image that you've attached to it (see "Editing contacts" later in this chapter).

Figure 3.4
Receiving a call while you're already on the phone.

If you don't want to interrupt your primary call, you can simply ignore the incoming call; it rolls to voice mail. If you *do* want to take the incoming call, follow these steps:

1. Press the Menu key to get the options shown at the bottom of **Figure 3.5**.

   You can either hold or end the call in progress while you answer the incoming call.

2. Tap the appropriate option, and talk to the second caller.

3. Press the red End key to end the second call.

   You'll be back on the line with the original caller—assuming, of course, that you tapped the "hold call in progress" option in Step 1. If you tapped the other option, sorry; I can't help you.

Figure 3.5
Press Menu to get options for incoming calls.

Voice mail

One consequence of the digital age is the proliferation of voice mail. Despite what the phone carriers tell you, however, it's unrealistic to expect to reach someone on her mobile phone any time, anywhere. As much as you may not want to believe it, people have families, jobs, and lives to deal with, and taking your phone call isn't always at the top of their list.

On one hand, voice mail can be frustrating. On the other hand, when it's combined with Caller ID, voice mail may be the single greatest privacy tool in the world. How many times has it saved you from taking a phone call at an inopportune time? You probably couldn't count them.

If you miss a call on your gPhone, a little status-bar alert tells you about it. You can either pull down the status bar to reveal the larger notification with the person's info (see Chapter 2 for a refresher on the status bar), or you can get the same information by pressing the Send key to launch the Dialer app and then tapping the Call Log tab at the top of the screen (refer to Figure 3.1).

When you receive a voice-mail message, another status-bar alert pops up. As with missed calls, pulling down the status bar gives you more information about the message, including the Caller ID information and the time when the call came in (**Figure 3.6**).

Figure 3.6
The notifications detail drawer displays a new voice mail and the associated missed call.

To retrieve a voice mail, just tap the status bar and slide it down; then tap the New Voicemail alert (refer to Figure 3.6). The key commands for saving and deleting voice mail vary from carrier to carrier (they're keys 9 and 7, respectively, on T-Mobile USA), so I'm not going to cover them in this book.

tip Tapping the voice-mail notification icon in the status bar is the fastest way to dial your voice mail.

note It's best to listen to the automated instructions all the way to the end when you first set up voice mail. This recording provides copious details on the carrier's voice-mail system, and it's good to take the time to learn all the options. Settle into a comfy chair and kick up your feet while you set up voice mail on your gPhone. Soon, the commands will become familiar, and before too long, they'll be second nature.

Call forwarding

Call forwarding isn't nearly as sexy as some of the other features, but it's quite handy nonetheless. Say you're taking a quick trip with your spouse, and you don't want to carry two phones. You can simply forward one phone's calls to the other. Heck, someone at Google must have thought that call forwarding is important, because this feature is listed in the Call Settings screen along with four other options (**Figure 3.7**). (I recommend that you leave the Operator Selection option alone unless you know what you're doing.)

Figure 3.7
Access call forwarding from this screen.

Simply tap the Call Forwarding option to display the gPhone's Call
Forwarding Settings screen (**Figure 3.8**). These settings let you do more
than simply set an Always Forward option, as you have to do on most
other mobile phones (including the iPhone). You can also choose to
forward calls when you're busy, unreachable, or just not answering the
phone. These settings are useful for business users and salespeople who
never want to miss a sales opportunity.

Figure 3.8
Call-forwarding
settings.

Tapping any call-forwarding setting displays a screen where you can
specify the number to which you want to forward your calls (**Figure 3.9**,
on the next page). You can also tap the silhouette icon next to the
phone-number field to choose one of your stored contacts' numbers.
I find this option most useful because the list of numbers that I can
recall easily is dwindling—another consequence of living in the digital
age, I guess.

Figure 3.9
Call-forwarding detail.

Keep in mind a couple of caveats about call forwarding, though:

- The G1 must be powered up to forward calls. If its battery runs out, calls are no longer forwarded.

- Calls forwarded to another phone rack up minutes on the forwarding phone, so if you forward calls from one mobile to another mobile, you'll be racking up minutes on *both* phones.

tip If your Google phone is lost or stolen, you can forward its calls to another phone by calling your carrier. T-Mobile customers can also manage their call-forwarding settings on MyT-Mobile.com.

Contacts

Although I say earlier in this chapter that the phone is the Google phone's most important feature, Contacts actually ties for first place. Without your contacts, how would you remember a person's phone number, e-mail address, or instant-messaging (IM) account? Contacts play a critical role on a mobile phone because they're your link to the outside world. They allow you to communicate with everyone who's important to you, which probably adds up to a lot of people. Businesspeople would argue that contacts are everything because they're sources of revenue. Personally, I just want to be able to call home to find out what's for dinner and see whether we need anything from the store.

People seem to change phone numbers, e-mail addresses, and street addresses more frequently than ever these days, though, so it's important to be vigilant about keeping your contact data current—if you want to actually reach anyone, that is. It's a never-ending task, which may be why Americans spend billions of dollars each year on contact management or customer relationship management (CRM) software.

If you have a Google phone, however, you can save that money, because another of the gPhone's many breakthrough features is its excellent data synchronization. Google has simplified the process tremendously by storing everything *on the cloud* (code for "on a Google server somewhere"), making it easier than ever to keep your ever-expanding contacts current. The process requires a little training and discipline, but storing your contact data on the cloud has two big payoffs:

- You can access it anywhere that you can get an Internet connection.

- It's virtually impossible to lose your data (unlike your phone, which you have a 50 percent chance of losing).

Managing contacts on the phone

You have two main ways to manage contacts on the Google phone:

 Launch the Dialer application by pressing the Send key, or tap the application icon in the home screen and then tap the Contacts tab.

 Launch the Contacts application in the home screen by tapping its icon.

Either way, you see your list of contacts, which you can add to or edit as I describe in the following sections.

When you're viewing the Contacts list, pressing Menu brings up four options (**Figure 3.10**):

Figure 3.10
Pressing the Menu key while viewing the Contacts list reveals four options at the bottom of the screen.

- **New Contact.** This option is pretty self-explanatory. Tap away on the gPhone's keyboard, and tap Save when you're finished.

- **Display Group.** This option allows you to view your contacts in more-manageable groups. You can limit your viewing to, say, contacts with phone numbers or contacts that you've starred (see the sidebar "Your All-Star Contacts" later in this chapter). Groups are great if you have a lot of contacts on your gPhone but don't need to see *all* of them. You create groups via the Google Contacts desktop Web interface (see "Managing contacts with Google Contacts" later in this chapter.)

- **Edit Sync Groups.** This option takes Display Group a step further, allowing you to narrow the number of contacts that are synced to your phone—just contacts that are starred or My Contacts, for example.

tip Limiting the number of contacts that you sync makes navigating your contacts faster and shortens sync time because less data is shuttling to and from the cloud.

- **Import Contacts.** This option reads any contacts that you have on your SIM (Subscriber Identity Module) card and allows you to import them selectively into Google Contacts. This feature can be handy for things like importing contacts from another phone that uses the Global System for Mobile communication (GSM) standard.

Adding contacts

A common social interaction these days involves whipping out a mobile phone to enter someone's phone number. It's the modern equivalent of exchanging business cards.

To add a new contact, follow these steps:

1. Launch the Dialer app (refer to "Incoming and outgoing calls" earlier in this chapter).

2. Tap Contacts > Menu > New Contact.

   The New Contact screen opens (**Figure 3.11**).

   Figure 3.11
   Android's New Contact screen. Enter as much detail as possible; even add a photo.

3. Fill in the appropriate details.

4. Optionally, tap the More Info button at the bottom of the screen to add new fields (depending on your tolerance for the Google phone's keyboard).

5. If you want, check the Send Calls Directly to Voicemail box so that all calls from this contact go straight to voice mail.

   This setting is a great defense against known telemarketers—especially the ones who call all the time to remind you that your car's warranty may be expiring.

6. Tap Save when you're finished.

> **tip** On the gPhone, the easiest way to add a new phone number is to dial that number (using Dialer, naturally), press Menu, and then tap Add to Contacts before you press Send.

Contacts entered on the gPhone are automagically synced to the Google cloud in the background—an amazingly useful and powerful feature.

Editing contacts

To edit or delete a contact, follow these steps:

1. Tap Dialer > Contacts to display your list of contacts.

2. Use the scroll tab on the right side of the screen to find the contact you want.

3. Tap a contact to display its information (**Figure 3.12**).

Figure 3.12
*Viewing an
existing contact.*

4. Press the Menu key to display contact-list options; then tap either Edit Contact or Delete Contact at the bottom of the screen.

Tapping Edit allows you to edit any of the fields for that contact (**Figure 3.13**).

Figure 3.13
*Editing an
existing contact.*

If you want to get fancy, you can add photos of your contacts to their contact information by tapping the framed-picture icon in the top-left corner of the Edit Contact screen (refer to Figure 3.11). Remember to tap Save when you're finished. Then, whenever you call your contacts or they call you, your gPhone will display their pictures. This feature is a nice personal touch but can take some time to set up, especially if you have a lot of contacts.

You can even assign individual ringtones to specific contacts. Just repeat Steps 1–3 earlier in this section; then tap Edit Contact, make a choice from the Ringtone drop-down menu, and tap Save.

Your All-Star Contacts

Although you may have hundreds—or even thousands—of contacts stored on your phone, odds are that you probably call about a dozen of them 80 percent of the time. To make it easy to find the friends and family members whom you call all the time, make them favorites. Think of the process as creating bookmarks or shortcuts for those contacts.

To create a favorite, just tap the star in the top-right corner of that person's contact screen (refer to Figure 3.12). This act places him in your short list (aka favorites) so that he's easy to find among the litany of barbecue, sushi, and Thai restaurants that you have stored on your gPhone. Favorites appear in their own speed-dial section of sorts on the fourth tab of the Dialer application (refer to Figure 3.1 earlier in this chapter).

You can star a contact in that person's Edit Contact screen on the Web as well as in the gPhone interface.

Managing contacts with Google Contacts

Real-time, online data synchronization isn't a trivial task. Many companies have failed miserably at it by underestimating what's involved and how complicated it really is. Someone once summed up the situation by saying, "Sync is hard."

But not Google. The gPhone synchronizes automatically with your data in Google Contacts (www.google.com/contacts) and Gmail (www.gmail.com) in the background.

Sync is a very powerful feature, and Google got it right with Android, providing it as a free service. How you use Google Contacts depends on whether you're starting from scratch or already using it. I discuss both approaches in the following sections.

Starting contacts from scratch

If you're new to Google, perhaps creating a new Google account just for your gPhone, you should take a bit of time to set up your contacts. As I mention earlier in this chapter, contacts are integral to your phone, and having them organized and up to date is essential to having a good gPhone experience.

Importing contacts

You can import any contacts in the CSV (comma-separated values) file format. The easiest way is to use the import tool in Google Contacts. Just follow these steps on your computer:

1. Log in to Google Contacts (www.google.com/contacts) from any Web browser.

2. Click the Import link in the top-right corner of the screen to open the My Contacts window (**Figure 3.14**).

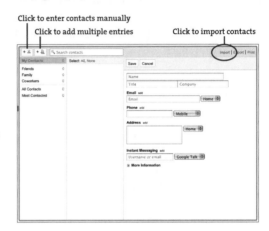

Figure 3.14
Adding a new contact with Google is easy. Just populate the fields in the My Contacts window, and add more when you run out.

3. Click the Browse button in the next window to navigate to and select your contact files.

4. Click Open.

5. Click Import.

If you're using Windows, you can import data from Microsoft Outlook, Outlook Express, Yahoo!, or Hotmail. Just export the contact data to a CSV file and then import that file into Google Contacts.

If you're using Address Book on a Mac, you have several ways to import contacts into Google:

- The simplest method is to choose Address Book > Preferences > General, check the Synchronize with Google check box, and then click the Google button. You'll be prompted to log in with your Google account, and Address Book will sync in the background.

- A free utility for the Mac called A to G (www.bborofka.com) exports a tidy CSV file to your desktop; this file imports easily into Google Contacts. The A to G utility is good for one-way migration to Google but doesn't offer syncing.

- An application called Spanning Sync (www.spanningsync.com; $25 for one year, $65 for a permanent license) allows Mac users to synchronize Address Book and iCal to Google Contacts and Calendars. The app may seem to be a little expensive, but it's worth the cost because it syncs bidirectionally (from Mac to Google, and vice versa) in the background.

Entering contacts manually

If you don't have a software application that Google Contacts can import contacts from, you can enter contacts directly by clicking the blue icon in the top-left corner of the Google Contacts window—the one showing one person next to a plus sign (refer to Figure 3.14 in the preceding section). Then just populate the fields, save your work, and move to the next contact.

> **tip** You can add multiple phone numbers and e-mail, street, and IM addresses by clicking the blue Add link next to each field name (refer to Figure 3.14). You can also add custom fields for notes and other things by clicking More Information at the bottom of the window.

Already using Google Contacts

If you're already using Gmail or Google Contacts as your primary contact manager, you're way ahead of the game. Your contacts already live on the cloud and are ready to go; in fact, they've probably downloaded to your gPhone already. Take a gander at the Contacts screen in the Dialer app (refer to "Managing contacts on the phone" earlier in this chapter). If you see contacts that you didn't add manually, you're in business. How easy was that?

Troubleshooting contacts

If you're not seeing your Google Contacts entries on your gPhone, here are a few things to check:

- Did you sign in on your phone under the same account that you use for Google Contacts? Getting the account sign-on right is imperative. If you have more than one Google account, you may find it easy to mix up those accounts.

- Are you in an area that has a solid data connection? Can you surf Web pages? If not, the problem is your Internet connection.

- If you set up your phone recently (as in hours ago), the contacts may not have fully synced from the cloud to your phone yet. Patience, Jedi, patience. Give it an hour or two.

tip Tip for the impatient: You can force the gPhone to sync with the cloud at any time by choosing Settings > Data Synchronization > Menu key > Sync Now.

After you've verified that your Google Contacts are synced between the cloud and your gPhone, you're all set! Now you can call, e-mail, IM, text (via Short Message Service [SMS]), or even map the address of any of your contacts directly from the phone—all of which I discuss in the next section.

Dialing, texting, e-mailing, and mapping a contact

Any time you're viewing a contact, you can contact that particular person or business in several ways, right from the contact screen. To the right of each piece of data (phone number, e-mail address, and so on) is an associated icon. As you've probably guessed, tapping that icon calls, messages, e-mails, or maps the contact that you're viewing. This feature is incredibly useful and centralizes all the ways to communicate with that contact.

The contact screen for Peachpit Press, my wonderful publisher, is a great example of a clean, well-populated screen (refer to Figure 3.12 earlier in this chapter). Having complete contact data like this example makes interacting with your contacts infinitely easier and faster, and it's well worth your investment in time.

Calendar

There's no question that the phone and Contacts features are integral parts of your mobile phone experience. I close the chapter with the third biggie: Calendar.

Calendar is very feature rich and frankly tough to beat, especially for the price. Google synchronizes its online calendars directly to Android phones over the air and completely free of charge. Many of the principles that I outline for Contacts earlier in this chapter apply to the Calendar application on the gPhone; also, the two applications are linked in many ways. (If you jumped directly to this section, I recommend that you read the "Contacts" section before proceeding.)

The concept is simple: You can manage calendar events on the gPhone itself or on the Web, depending on what suits you. Most people find it easier to enter and manage their calendars on a desktop computer because of the familiar keyboard and large screen. gPhone syncing is bidirectional, so you can edit in either place, or both, and Google keeps both calendars in sync.

As with Google Contacts, the way you use Google Calendar depends on whether you're starting from scratch or already using it. I cover both methods in the next two sections.

Starting a calendar from scratch

If you're new to Google or just created a new Google account for use with your gPhone, you should take some time to set up your calendars. Like the phone and contacts, calendars are integral to the gPhone experience, and having your mobile calendar organized will make you more productive.

Entering calendar events manually

The easiest way to enter calendar events is via the Web interface. Follow these steps on your computer:

1. Log in to Google Calendar (www.google.com/calendar) from any Web browser.

2. Click the Create Event link in the top-left corner of the screen (**Figure 3.15**).

Click to create an event

Figure 3.15
Events are easy to create in the Google Calendar Web interface.

3. Fill in the fields and set the options.

   For details, see "Working with events and reminders" later in this chapter.

4. Click Save.

Importing calendar events

If you already maintain a calendar in iCal or Microsoft Outlook, you can import it into Google Calendar with the handy online import tool (www. google.com/calendar). The only catch is that event information must be in iCal or CSV format. If you're using a calendar program that doesn't export to one of those formats, you need to export the calendar data to a format that Google Calendar can read.

To import calendar data into Google Calendar from a desktop computer, tap Add > Import Calendar; click the Add link in the Other Calendars section in the bottom-left corner of the screen (**Figure 3.16**); and then browse to the file that you exported from your previous calendar application.

Click to import calendar data

Figure 3.16
*You can import
data into Google
Calendar.*

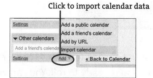

If you're new to Google Calendar, now would be a good time to familiarize yourself with the full version on your desktop computer at your own pace. The balance of this chapter focuses primarily on calendars on the gPhone.

Already using Google Calendar

If you're already using Google Calendar, pat yourself on the back, put your feet up, and maybe even take an afternoon nap. Your calendar events are already on the cloud and may already be synced to your gPhone!

Launch the Calendar application on the gPhone. If it looks like **Figure 3.17**, you're in business. Your calendar is already synced. If it's blank, with no little color bar on the right edge of each date, either you have a very light month planned or your calendar isn't synced (see the "Troubleshooting contacts" section earlier in this chapter; those tips also apply to calendars).

Figure 3.17
A well-populated month view on the gPhone's Calendar screen.

After you've verified that your Google Calendar data is synced between the cloud and your gPhone, you're ready to roll. You can view your calendars, create events, and receive reminders.

Viewing a calendar

People most commonly use Google Calendar simply to view a calendar. About 90 percent of the calendaring I do on my phone is checking what's coming up today, this week, and this month. Usually, when a friend asks something like "Are you available on August 7 to see Phish at the Gorge?", I'll whip out my phone, fire up Calendar, and zoom to that date.

tip Scroll between months by swiping your finger up and down the screen.

Pressing the Menu key while you're in the Calendar application (conveniently located in the application drawer) gives you options to view a day, week, or month at a time (**Figure 3.18**). Month view can get kind of cramped on the G1's small screen, but luckily, tapping a day switches you to day view, where you can read the details about events.

Figure 3.18
Calendar options.

Using other calendars

Your calendar is very important because it allows you to make meetings and your kid's swimming lesson on time—but that's only the beginning. Google also allows you to create and maintain multiple calendars for things like clubs, groups, and sports leagues that you're involved in. One amazingly useful feature lets you view your significant other's calendar. Just have him or her set up a calendar in Google and then click Add a Friend's Calendar in the Other Calendars section (refer to Figure 3.16 earlier in this chapter).

Also, you can sign up for an assortment of public calendars by choosing Add > Browse Calendars (**Figure 3.19**, on the next page). Calendars for everything from U.S. to international holidays and fun things like phases of the moon are accessible from the Google Calendar Web interface.

Figure 3.19
A small selection of the public calendars that you can subscribe to (for free) in Google Calendars.

tip I recommend setting up separate calendars for your work and personal events so that your vet appointments and sales meetings don't mix. Don't worry, though; you can still overlay all your calendars on one master calendar and view everything at the same time. Keeping separate calendars is best because it allows you to toggle the work calendar off while you're away on vacation and share only personal events with your family members (who couldn't care less about your next sales meeting, thankyouverymuch!).

You can control which calendars you see on the gPhone by pressing the Menu key and then tapping More > My Calendars (**Figure 3.20**).

Figure 3.20
The My Calendars screen lets you choose which Google Calendars you view on your gPhone.

My Calendars allows you to toggle the display of calendars on and off by checking and clearing check boxes to the left of those calendars' names. A green check means that the calendar is being displayed on your phone; a gray check means that it *isn't* being displayed (as weird as that sounds).

You can add and delete calendars by pressing the Menu key while you're in the My Calendars screen. You'll see two buttons at the bottom of the screen for—what else?—adding and removing calendars. Didn't I tell you that this was going to be easy?

Working with events and reminders

When a friend asks whether you're available on a certain day, and you discover that you are by checking your calendar, it's best to create a new event right there on the spot. Sure, it's easy to say that you'll remember the event and put it in your calendar later, but if you're like me, doing that is virtually impossible. If I don't enter an event in my calendar right away, it usually doesn't happen. Taking time to create a new event *the minute that it's confirmed* will pay off down the road.

You have two primary ways to create events (or appointments, or meetings) on the gPhone:

- Tap Calendar > Menu > New Event.
- Tap and hold a specific day and time in any of the calendar views (day, week, or month).

Either method brings up the Event Details screen (**Figure 3.21**, on the next page). Just complete a few of the whos and whats about the event, and tap Save. The new event immediately appears on your gPhone calendar and synchronizes with the desktop version of Google Calendar within a few minutes.

Figure 3.21
Viewing calendar
event details.

Reminders are important aspects of the whole event-creation process and therefore worth reviewing. When you add a new event, by default the phone is set to give you a lowly 10-minute reminder, which isn't enough time to make it to the dry cleaner's down the street, let alone to catch a flight. You can set reminders any time you create or edit a calendar event (on the phone or on the Web) as far as a week out, but I usually choose a 2-hour reminder for local events, which allows me enough time for preparation and travel.

 Reminder icons appear in the status bar and can be expanded to show more detail.

Setting the Agenda

If the day, week, and month views aren't your cup of tea, you're not alone. The month and week views can get cluttered and hard to read pretty quickly if you have more than three events per day (not as hard as it sounds). Fear not, fair reader! Google has a solution for that problem too: the Agenda (**Figure 3.22**).

Figure 3.22
The Agenda list is easiest to view and most legible when you have lots of events and/or calendars.

The Agenda is essentially a list view of all your upcoming events from all synced calendars, displayed in a nice clean interface. It shows the name of the event, the date(s), location, alarm, URL, repeating status (the circling-arrows icon), and the calendar color. Tap an event in any view to view and edit the event details (**Figure 3.23**).

Figure 3.23
The Agenda's View Event screen provides a little more information than list view.

The Agenda is by far the easiest calendar view to read and use, which is probably why it's the first option you see when you press the Menu key in the Calendar app. You'll use it a lot. I rarely look at the other calendar views because it's so much quicker to flick and scroll through the Agenda.

Caveat Calendar

Like many other things in life, Google Calendar does have a couple of limitations:

- As with most Google applications, I find it quicker to do any substantial editing in the full version of the application on a desktop computer. For entering anything more than a few words, I'm much faster at typing on my full desktop keyboard than on any mobile device's keyboard, and nothing beats a big screen, especially when I'm trying to view a busy month view in Google Calendar.

- At this writing, several features of the desktop version of Google Calendar haven't made it to the Android edition: sending invitations, creating calendars, sharing calendars, and adding a public calendar.

I wouldn't worry too much about these limitations, though. All the important features are in the Android edition now, and a lot of talented coders at Google headquarters are on the case. I wouldn't be surprised if Google Calendar could paint your house by the time you read this book.

So that wraps up a pretty long chapter about the Google phone's three core applications: the phone, Contacts, and Calendar. As with anything, you'll get more proficient with use, so it's important to embrace these three core apps and put them to work for you. Time invested in them now will pay off in more free time in the future—or at least in fewer missed meetings.

In Chapter 4, I take a break from the software side to review the Google phone's powerful hardware—specifically, its 3G, Wi-Fi, and Bluetooth radios.

4

On the Radios

In this chapter, I dig into a few of the Google phone's key hardware features—specifically, its radios. *Radios* are the chips that the gPhone uses for communicating via 3G, Wi-Fi, Global Positioning System (GPS), and Bluetooth. For the most part, these radios work invisibly, doing their thing silently in the background, but learning some subtle nuances of their interfaces can be helpful.

Although the topic can get a little technical, this chapter provides lots of information about the gPhone's various radios, including the most important tip of all: how to turn them off to conserve battery life. I explore the features and benefits of four of the gPhone's radios, and show you how to maximize their performance.

If you don't particularly like to tinker with things like settings and configuration screens, this chapter may not be for you. Feel free to skip ahead to the chapters on fun aspects of the phone (such as software), if that's more your speed.

3G

The Google phone, at this writing, is based on the third generation (3G) of telecommunication hardware standards. 3G phones use advanced chips to communicate with transmitters on carriers' radio towers to move data and voice packets back and forth more quickly and efficiently.

As you might expect, 3G phones are better than *2G* phones, but you won't notice the difference immediately while using one of them. You'll see the biggest difference between 3G and 2G (or, more accurately, 2.5G) phones when you use Internet-intensive applications that stream audio and video to your phone. 3G is simply capable of passing more data back and forth than 2G is, so the Internet feels much faster on a 3G phone.

3G devices can achieve data-transfer rates of up to 14.4 megabits per second (Mbps) on the downlink and 5.8 Mbps on the uplink. This speed is much faster than the lowly 2.5G (aka GPRS) standard that it replaces. 2.5G data rates vary from 56 to 114 kilobits per second (Kbps)— a slow speed that makes using the Internet on a mobile phone almost intolerable.

tip 3G coverage varies by city and depends on the carrier. You can check your carrier's 3G coverage by going to its Web site and searching for a coverage map. You can find the T-Mobile USA coverage map at www.t-mobile.com/coverage/.

One thing to keep in mind is that print publishing represents a moment in time, and at this particular moment (May 2009), plans are under way for an even faster 4G network, capable of reaching speeds of 100 Mbps on a moving smartphone and 1 gigabit per second (Gbps!) on a stationary smartphone.

3G acronyms

Although this information may be overkill for some readers, I think it's a good idea to give you a quick overview of the various technical acronyms associated with the Google phone.

Preceding each acronym in **Table 4.1** (on the next page) is the notification icon that pops up in the status bar when you're using that particular radio. (Read more about the status bar in Chapter 2.)

Power-draw issues

The most important thing to keep in mind with the 3G radio in the Google phone is that it draws more power than the 2G radio. So there's a downside to slurping down all those delectable Internet bits at blazing speeds: shorter battery life. The more you use the radios in the gPhone, the shorter your battery life will be. It's as simple as that.

This same principle goes for all of the radios in the gPhone: The more you use them, the more power they will drain from your battery. Conservation rules the roost.

Table 4.1 Wireless Acronyms

ICON	ACRONYM/TRANSLATION

GSM (Global System for Mobile communications)
GSM is a second-generation (2G) mobile phone system used by more than 3 billion people in more than 212 countries and territories, and usually is voice-only.

GPRS (General Packet Radio Service)
Think of GPRS as being the data side of GSM, with speeds between 56 and 114 Kbps.

EDGE (Enhanced Data rates for GSM Evolution)
This technology provides improved data transmission rates on top of standard GPRS. Data rates range from 400 Kbps to 1 Mbps.

3G (third generation)
The third generation of telecommunication hardware standards is capable of generating data throughput of up to 14.4 Mbps.

Wi-Fi (wireless fidelity)
Wi-Fi usually is the fastest Internet access option, faster even than 3G. Speeds can vary widely, however, depending on the wireless access point you're connected to. I cover Wi-Fi in detail later in this chapter.

GPS (Global Positioning System)
GPS satellites help your phone calculate its longitude and latitude. Then the phone uses this information to pinpoint your location on a map. I review all kinds of other cool stuff that GPS does later in this chapter.

note If you're a fan of automotive GPS receivers from Garmin, don't forget to pick up a copy of my *Garmin nüvi Pocket Guide*, also from Peachpit Press.

For reasons that should be obvious, your phone's battery life can be a safety issue. You need to keep a close eye on your battery-management techniques to maximize battery life, especially while you're traveling. If you're going to be away from power for a long period—going hiking, camping, or rock climbing, for example—and need to rely on your phone for safety, it's imperative to save battery power by downshifting from 3G to 2G networks (**Figure 4.1**). You should also disable the Wi-Fi and Bluetooth radios by tapping Settings > Wireless Controls (**Figure 4.2**) to conserve your battery for those critical times when you need it—like calling for a ride home!

Figure 4.1

Android's Mobile Network Settings screen allows you to use only 2G networks to save battery life.

Figure 4.2

Clear the Wi-Fi and Bluetooth check boxes to conserve battery power.

note Before disabling 3G, keep in mind that it has many advantages over 2G. 3G provides faster mobile Internet and better call quality; it also allows data and calls to occur simultaneously. When you drop down to 2G, you can't access the Internet and use the phone at the same time.

Another way to save battery life is to tap Settings > Sound and Display; then, in the Display Settings section (bottom of **Figure 4.3**), set both Brightness and Screen Timeout as low as possible. (The minimum Screen Timeout setting is 15 seconds.)

Figure 4.3

The Display Settings options (bottom) let you reduce screen brightness and the screen-timeout interval to conserve battery power.

tip If you're particularly anxious about battery life, remember to turn off the screen by pressing the End key as soon as you finish using the phone. Don't wait for the screen timeout to kick in.

Conservation software

If you don't like having to dig through multiple layers of menus to find the Google phone's radio settings, download Useful Switchers from the Android Market (see Chapter 7). This $3 app allows you to toggle all the gPhone's radios on and off from one handy screen (**Figure 4.4**). Download it directly from the gPhone, or read more about it on the developer's Web site: www.maximyudin.com/mysoftware.

Figure 4.4
An extended screen shot (the actual screen isn't this long) of Useful Switchers, which lets you adjust the gPhone's various radios from one convenient location.

Another great application is Locale (**Figure 4.5**), from two forty four a.m. (www.twofortyfouram.com). Locale takes conservation up a notch by managing all your phone's settings dynamically, based on conditions such as location and time. With this app, you can specify a situation in which you never want your phone to ring—while you're in court, for example, based on what time you're in court or even where the court is located.

Figure 4.5
Locale takes settings management to the extreme, allowing you to control how your phone behaves based on preset situations.

Locale can change your phone settings based on your location data, which it gathers from your gPhone's numerous radios. You can set a profile of settings for your phone to be enabled as soon as you come within range of your company's Wi-Fi network, for example, and another profile to be activated when you're on your home network.

You can also set up a Low Battery profile that turns off all but the essential gPhone radios when battery power drops below a certain threshold—say, 20 percent.

Finally, if you're always missing calls when your phone is set to vibrate or mute mode, try Locale's VIP mode. It ensures that certain phone calls (such as those from the day-care center or your doctor) always ring through, even when your phone is in mute or silent mode.

Wi-Fi

There's no question that the Internet is a huge part of our lives, in part as a direct result of the proliferation of wireless access. In the not-too-distant past, accessing the Internet meant sitting down in front of a computer with a fixed network connection wired to a wall. Those wires went only so far, however, which meant that your surfing session expired as soon as you got up from the chair. Well, no more.

Since the invention of the wireless Internet router, you're no longer required to be tethered to an Ethernet or RJ11 cable plugged into the wall. You can use an inexpensive wireless router to surf the Internet from the couch, kitchen, or bedroom with ease. Now that wireless Internet access is everywhere (or so it seems), many gadgets come with wireless radios built in.

The Android phone is no exception. In fact, it's practically a requirement for a smartphone (does anyone else dislike that term?) to have wireless, or *Wi-Fi*, capabilities. In November 2008, Research In Motion (RIM) and Verizon Wireless released the BlackBerry Storm *without* Wi-Fi and were universally panned by critics (including me) for the omission.

Using Wi-Fi

Like most things on the gPhone, Wi-Fi isn't very complicated to set up. Just tap Settings > Wireless Controls to access the Wireless Controls screen, where you can set up everything you need to access a Wi-Fi network at your home or office (**Figure 4.6**). When Wi-Fi access is set up, your preferred wireless access points are stored on the Google phone, so you can pretty much set it and forget it. Next time you're within range of a Wi-Fi access point that you've connected to before, the gPhone will switch from 3G or EDGE to the faster Wi-Fi.

Figure 4.6
The Wireless Controls screen allows you to see at a glance which Wi-Fi access point you're connected to. Here, I'm connected to an access point called Fluffhead.

To connect to a Wi-Fi network, tap Settings > Wireless Controls > Wi-Fi Settings and then tap one of the listed networks in the Wi-Fi Networks section (**Figure 4.7**, on the next page). Networks that are encrypted with a password (like Fluffhead in Figure 4.7) display a lock over the Wi-Fi icon and require you to enter a password to gain access. Open networks (such as Fluffhead Guest in the figure) don't require a password and show the basic Wi-Fi icon sans lock.

Figure 4.7
The Wi-Fi Settings screen allows you to connect a Wi-Fi network.

If you want to connect to a network that's not in the list, just tap Add a Wi-Fi Network at the bottom of the Wi-Fi Networks section; then enter its Service Set ID (SSID) and choose an option from the Security drop-down menu (**Figure 4.8**). If the wireless network has security, the next screen will prompt you to enter your password.

Figure 4.8
Adding a Wi-Fi network is easy, but you must know its SSID and security information, which you enter here.

When you're connected to a Wi-Fi access point, you see an icon in the status bar. The four segments in the icon indicate how strong your connection is. A Wi-Fi icon with a question mark over it indicates a problem with the wireless connection.

Taking precautions

To wrap up this section, I want to leave you with a little anecdote about Wi-Fi security. In short, don't trust unknown networks with your confidential information. It's trivial to create a network called Starbucks, McDonald's, or Hilton Honors and then monitor the traffic of anyone who connects to it. The practice is called *spoofing*. A spoofed network is designed to look and operate like a normal Wi-Fi network, with one nefarious difference: The person who set it up could be scanning the traffic flowing through it for potentially valuable information.

If you plop down in a comfy chair in your favorite coffee shop and connect to the first free wireless access point that pops up, you could be connected to the laptop of the guy next to you, and he could be capturing your login information as you access your online bank account.

Not all free wireless access points are set up by hackers to steal your information, of course. My point is that you must use common sense when using unknown Wi-Fi networks. Surfing the Web is pretty safe on a wireless network, for example, but logging in to your e-mail account can expose your login credentials to a baddie. I'd refrain from logging in to any financial Web site (bank, credit union, investments, and so on) whatsoever while you're logged in to a Wi-Fi network that you don't know. It's just not worth the risk.

tip **Change your passwords often, and use different passwords for different sites. Most people rarely change their passwords, and some use the same password for all the Web sites they access. Does this sound like you? You could be risking the security of your identity, because once baddies have your password, they can do a lot of damage with it. A friendly warning: Don't be promiscuous in your wireless surfing habits.**

GPS

Definitely one of the most enjoyable aspects of the Google phone is the Global Positioning System (GPS) functionality that's built into many models. As I mention in the introduction, numerous Android-powered phones will be on the market by the time you read this book, each with a different set of features. Check with your carrier to see whether your Google phone has GPS.

Activating GPS

You can turn the GPS feature on and off, but the setting is tucked away where you might not think to look. Tap Settings > Security & Location to access the My Location Sources screen, where you'll find the Enable GPS Satellites option (**Figure 4.9**).

Figure 4.9
*Simply check
or uncheck the
Enable GPS
Satellites box,
depending on
your mood that
day.*

If you're not a heavy user, I recommend keeping GPS on all the time, because it adds a new dimension of utility to your phone (as you see in this section). When this feature isn't in use (that is, you're not actively using My Location or the directions features), the GPS chip goes into low-power mode. When you're using the gPhone for real-time directions, however, GPS is a battery hog; in fact, it's one of the biggest draws of power on the Google phone.

A little common sense goes a long way. If you're planning an all-day walk, hike, or bike ride—or any other event that will have you away from power for an extended period—it's best to turn off all unnecessary radios (like GPS) unless you need them. (See my battery-conservation tips in "Power-draw issues" earlier in this chapter.)

Using GPS creatively

If you think that GPS is useful in automotive applications, it's even more useful (is that possible?) in a handheld device. The first and most common use of a GPS chip is to get directions from point A to point B, which is an incredibly powerful feature. Millions of drivers rely on GPS every day to get them to their destinations. In a mobile device, GPS is especially useful for getting directions while you're on foot or on public transit (see "Google Maps" later in this chapter).

Besides getting directions, you can use GPS technology in several fun and creative ways, thanks to the following third-party applications. All these apps are available in the Android Market, which I cover in detail in Chapter 7:

- Measure the distance between two locations within 10 feet or so (GPSMeasure)

- Find your car in an airport or mall parking lot (Car Finder)

- Record the exact path of a run or bike ride (RunnerTrainer and RideTrac)

- Use your phone as a speedometer (Speed Proof)

- Find the cheapest gas prices (GasBot)

- Measure the distance to the pin from where you're standing on the golf course (TeeDroid Caddy)

- Participate in *geocaching,* an outdoor treasure-hunting game in which the participants use GPS devices (Orienteer)

- Locate traffic and safety cameras (Traffic Cams)

My current favorite GPS application is FindMyPhone, which helps you locate your gPhone if you lose it. If you have this application installed, and you misplace your phone, just send the phone a special SMS text message (from another phone, obviously). Your lost phone will reply with its current location so that you can go recover it. Brilliant! If only I could use this application for my house keys!

Google Maps

 One of the most powerful applications in Android is Google Maps Mobile (also called *Google Maps* or simply *Maps* on the gPhone). When it's combined with a built-in GPS chip and an accelerometer, which knows which way you're holding or tilting the phone, the Maps application can find your current location on a map to an accuracy of about 10 feet (3 meters). Pretty powerful stuff.

The advent of live mobile maps means never having to use a paper map again—provided that you don't run out of battery power, that is! With Google Maps, you can determine your current location, find businesses and landmarks, get driving directions and real-time traffic reports, and explore satellite and street images.

Google Maps is probably worthy of its own chapter (or possibly even its own book), but because I don't have the space for full coverage here, I'll focus on some of its key features.

The basics

When you launch Google Maps for Android, the app displays the last map you viewed. If you have GPS turned on, Maps can pinpoint your exact location; just press the Menu key and then tap My Location (**Figure 4.10**).

Figure 4.10
You can access most of the options in Maps when you press the Menu key.

You access specific functions by tapping any of the following buttons, which appear after you press the Menu key:

- **Search.** Find an address or city by tapping Search—or even just search for pizza, and Maps returns all the pizza shops near you, neatly plotted on a map. For retail establishments that it finds, Maps also lists their complete street addresses and phone numbers. Pizza indeed!

- **Directions.** This feature is Google Maps at its best, giving you directions from point A to point B. If you've used online mapping before, the Directions feature will be very familiar to you. If not, enter your

start and end locations, and tap Route (**Figure 4.11**) to get directions
(**Figure 4.12**). It's really that simple.

Figure 4.11
*Getting directions
is as easy as
entering two
locations and
then tapping
Route.*

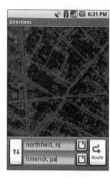

Figure 4.12
*Follow the
written directions
here, or tap Show
Map to see the
route plotted on
a map.*

tip   Tap the square button to the right of each address field to choose
a location source (**Figure 4.13**), which allows you to quickly select
My Current Location as a starting point and a contact's location (or even a
bookmark called History) as the destination. Look, Ma, no typing!

Figure 4.13
*Set a location
source in this
screen.*

- **Map Mode.** The Map Mode screen (**Figure 4.14**) lets you choose a map-viewing option: Map, Satellite, Traffic, or Street View. (I cover the latter two views in detail in the next section.)

Figure 4.14
*Map Mode allows
you to choose
how you want
to view a map. In
the background is
Satellite mode.*

- **My Location.** This feature asks the GPS satellites for your longitude and latitude and then plots the intersection of those points on a map (a Google Map, naturally).

- **Latitude.** Tapping the Latitude button takes you to Google Latitude (www.google.com/latitude), a social-networking service that plots your friends' locations on a map—a handy way to see who's out and about. Then you can text, instant-message, or call any of those people. This feature is only as good as the number of your friends who use it, however.

note If you're concerned about stalkers, keep in mind that Latitude is an opt-in feature, which means that *you* turn it on and *you* determine who can see your location.

- **More.** Tapping the More button reveals additional Maps options (**Figure 4.15**) that let you clear the map, zoom, and even view the map history (your previous searches). If you're concerned about the privacy implications of GPS, the privacy option lets you choose one of four privacy levels, ranging from sending automatic location updates to turning Latitude off.

Figure 4.15
Tap the More button to see extra options.

Traffic and Street views

The Map Mode screen (refer to Figure 4.14) allows you to choose any of four ways to view your maps. You should be familiar with the map and satellite options, which are the most common choices. But the power of Google Maps really shines through in the last two choices:

- **Traffic.** Traffic mode displays real-time traffic overlaid on top of your current map or route—great for finding the fastest route.

- **Street View.** This amazing mode shows street-level images of your map location (**Figure 4.16**). Because Street View is labor-intensive, requiring Google personnel to take and upload millions of photos, it's not available everywhere, but it is available for many major cities in the United States and abroad.

Figure 4.16
A Street View image of Paris, displayed in a Web browser.

> **tip** Before you book a hotel in a new place, look up the address on Google Maps and then check out the exterior of the hotel property via Street View. This feature is a great way to scope out a neighborhood before booking your room—although it works better on a nice large computer screen than it does on your mobile phone's screen.

At press time, Google Maps for Android didn't include walking or public-transit information, but because these features are available on other mobile phones, it should be only a matter of time before they're available for Android. After all, Android is Google's own mobile operating system!

tip If the navigation features included in Google Maps are too pedestrian (pun intended) for you, consider upgrading to TeleNav GPS for Android. It's available in Android Market (see Chapter 7) and on the TeleNav Web site (www.telenav.com). TeleNav costs $10 per month and turns your phone into a stand-alone GPS receiver with some features that aren't available in other phones, including 3D maps, voice recognition for hands-free operation, live traffic updates, and a large database of points of interest that include restaurant reviews and gas prices.

Bluetooth

Bluetooth—an open wireless protocol for exchanging data over short distances—seems like it was invented for mobile phones. Compared with the 3G and Wi-Fi radios in the Google phone, which are designed primarily for Internet access, Bluetooth has a short range. The theoretical range for Bluetooth 2.0 with Enhanced Data Rate (EDR) is about 33 feet (10 meters), but in practice, it's more like 10 to 20 feet.

Bluetooth has many uses, such as creating personal area networks (PANs) and sharing data between devices, but its primary application in mobile phones is wireless headsets. I cover the various applications of Bluetooth in the following sections.

Headsets

Although they make us look like Borgs wandering around talking to ourselves, Bluetooth headsets have become part of the technology landscape. There's no denying the convenience of being able to talk to someone on a mobile phone completely hands-free; it expands the freedom that started with cordless phones at home. The difference, of course, is that instead of being able to wander around our houses yapping, now we can walk just about anywhere in the world yapping.

Setting up a Bluetooth headset in Android is simple. After you initially *pair* (link) your headset and your Google phone, the phone will remember the settings so that you don't have to repeat the pairing exercise each time you want to use your headset.

To get started, follow these steps:

1. Tap Settings > Wireless Controls to display the Wireless Controls screen, which includes Bluetooth and Bluetooth Settings options (**Figure 4.17**).

   You can tell at a glance whether Bluetooth is turned on; if it is, you'll see a check in its check box.

Figure 4.17
Wireless Controls allows you to toggle Wi-Fi, Bluetooth, and Airplane mode on and off.

2. If Bluetooth isn't turned on, tap the check box to enable it.

3. Tap the Bluetooth Settings option to open the Bluetooth Settings screen (**Figure 4.18**, on the next page).

   The Bluetooth Devices section of this screen is where all the action happens. Here, you'll see any Bluetooth devices that are within range of your phone and discoverable. If your headset isn't listed, make sure that it's in discoverable mode (if you're not sure how to do this,

consult your headset's user manual for instructions) and then tap
Menu > Scan for Devices.

Figure 4.18
*Android's
Bluetooth
Settings screen.*

4. When you see your headset in the Bluetooth Devices list (mine is
   called Jawbone in Figure 4.18), tap it.

5. If you're prompted for a personal identification number (PIN) for your
   headset (**Figure 4.19**), enter that code to gain access to your device.

   Consult your manual for your particular device's PIN, or search for it
   on Google.

Figure 4.19
*Most Bluetooth
devices require
a PIN.*

Many Bluetooth headsets I've used have a PIN of 0000 or 1234, so if you're stuck, those codes are good places to start.

 When Bluetooth is on, you'll see an icon in the status bar. The left icon in the margin here indicates that Bluetooth is on; the right icon indicates that you're connected to a Bluetooth device.

Like the other three radios covered in this chapter, Bluetooth drains battery quickly when it's enabled, although not as quickly as GPS, Wi-Fi, and 3G do (in that order). It's important to practice good conservation techniques and use Bluetooth sparingly when you're away from power for long stretches of time.

note **Always use a wired or wireless headset when you use your phone while driving; in many states, it's the law.**

Mind Your Mobile Manners

Although they have obvious safety benefits, such as allowing you to use a mobile phone while driving, Bluetooth headsets aren't a license to forget your manners and common courtesy. It's important to respect other people's personal space while you're in public. Too many people babble on their Bluetooth headsets (and mobile phones) at full register with no concern for the people around them. Don't be that person! End your call when you're around other people (especially in confined spaces) or at least keep your voice down.

Other Bluetooth profiles

Bluetooth isn't limited to wireless headsets—well, sort of. Bluetooth is all about *profiles*—wireless interface specifications for communication among Bluetooth devices. As I write this chapter, the T-Mobile G1 supports only the Hands-Free Profile (HFP) and doesn't support stereo Bluetooth, also known as A2DP (Advanced Audio Distribution Profile). This means that you can't stream music from your gPhone to a pair of wireless stereo headphones over Bluetooth. Neither can you connect to wireless keyboards or transfer files over Bluetooth. The only Bluetooth accessories that the G1 supports out of the box are wireless headsets and hands-free kits. As with all software from our favorite company in Mountain View, however, this situation is certain to change.

note The stereo Bluetooth (A2DP) and Audio/Video Remote Control Profile (AVRCP) profiles were added to the Bluetooth stack in development builds of the Android OS, code-named Cupcake, which means that they should be available by the time you read this book. When they are, you'll be able to use stereo headsets and even use your gPhone as a Bluetooth remote control.

Currently, 28 Bluetooth profiles are available, each with a different application. Several other mobile phones on the market already support additional Bluetooth profiles (especially A2DP), and it's only a matter of time before the Google phone does as well.

Keep in mind that the G1 is the first Android phone released and certainly will get improvements down the road. Also, the Bluetooth implementation on your Google phone depends on the hardware manufacturer and the carrier. Some handset manufacturers (HTC, in the case of the G1) limit the phone's Bluetooth capabilities; others limit the Bluetooth options available. Check the Bluetooth specs on your particular gPhone by going to the carrier's Web site and drilling down into the specs for your specific phone.

5

E-Mail, Messaging, and Web

Now that I've given you some technical background on the radios inside your Google phone, I want to turn your attention to some of the more practical applications of the device. Undoubtedly, one of the primary reasons you purchased a gPhone is to send and receive e-mail on it. E-mail is one of the defining features of a smartphone, and if your Google phone has a QWERTY keyboard (as the G1 does), soon you'll be tapping out e-mails almost as fast as you can on your desktop computer.

In this chapter, I take a close look at the ins and outs of e-mail and messaging. I round out the chapter with a look at the gPhone's excellent Web browser.

E-Mail

The Google phone allows you to take your e-mail with you wherever you go, making it even more convenient than on a desktop or notebook computer. The gPhone actually comes with two e-mail applications: Gmail and Email (**Figure 5.1**). The first is Google's Webmail service, which is widely regarded as being one of the best; the second is a universal e-mail client that you can use to access any e-mail account based on POP3 or IMAP.

Figure 5.1
Android's Gmail and Email applications help you stay in touch while on the go.

Gmail

Email

 note POP3 (Post Office Protocol, Version 3) and IMAP (Internet Message Access Protocol) are the dominant e-mail protocols.

Using Gmail

Google began offering Webmail service under the Gmail moniker publicly in 2007, although it was available as a private beta application as early as 2004. The service has since grown to more than 100 million accounts, largely because of its simple yet powerful interface and high storage capacity (currently, 7 GB per account). It's also desirable for people who receive large attachments because a Gmail account will accept attachments as large as 20 MB—double the capacity of its competitors.

In addition to being intuitive enough for my 78-year-old mother-in-law to use, Gmail is loaded with features such as a powerful search feature (no surprise there!) and a threaded view called *conversations* that allows you to see all messages with the same subject in one convenient screen without having to hunt through your inbox for previous messages on the same topic.

The main Gmail view is the inbox, which lists all your messages in reverse chronological order (**Figure 5.2**).

Figure 5.2
The Gmail inbox.

The most powerful feature of Gmail on Android shows new messages in your inbox as they arrive without your having to refresh the inbox or check your e-mail. This feature, called *push,* means that your Gmail inbox is up to date at all times.

Launching the app

Because Gmail is tied to the Google account that you set up in Chapter 2, you don't have anything to set up. Just launch the application by tapping its icon, and you're greeted by your inbox.

As you accumulate e-mails in your account, you'll see your most recent e-mails in the first screen. To see older e-mails, just drag your finger up the screen, a technique called *flicking*.

Reading an e-mail is as simple as tapping it in the inbox (**Figure 5.3**). When you do, you see the subject line, sender, and date, followed by the message itself.

Figure 5.3
Gmail displays beautifully on the gPhone. Did you really expect anything less?

> **note** At this writing, the Gmail application is limited to one account: the primary account that you set up on the phone in Chapter 2. If you need to access multiple Gmail accounts on the gPhone, you can set up the others as POP3 or IMAP accounts in the Email application, which I discuss later in the chapter.

Because Gmail can display HTML messages, e-mails are rendered beautifully on the gPhone via *antialiasing,* a technology that generates smooth round edges and easy-to-read, eye-pleasing text. Tap the star to the right of the sender's e-mail address to mark the message as a favorite, as you can do with contacts (see Chapter 3).

Viewing inbox options

Tapping the Menu key while you're viewing the inbox gives you access
to the five options shown in **Figure 5.4**.

Figure 5.4
*To access Gmail
options, press the
Menu key while
you're viewing
the inbox.*

These options are

- **Refresh.** For the truly impatient, this option forces the inbox to refresh
  (although it technically isn't required, thanks to Gmail's push feature).

- **Compose.** Tap this button to write a new e-mail.

- **View Labels.** This option, which is another way to filter your e-mail,
  displays only e-mail with a given label (see "Managing mail" later in
  this chapter).

- **Search.** Allows you to search your e-mail for a keyword or phrase.

- **Settings.** Gives you access to further options in the General Settings
  screen (**Figure 5.5**, on the next page):

  - **Signature.** Allows you to add a custom footer to messages that you
    compose. Usually, a signature contains contact information.

  - **Confirm Delete.** Displays a confirmation dialog box when you mark
    an e-mail for deletion (see "Managing mail" later in this chapter).

- **Labels.** Lets you specify which labels are synchronized to your gPhone.

@ - **Email Notifications.** Displays a status-bar icon when you receive a new e-mail.

> **tip** I highly recommend that you keep this option enabled; it's super-convenient.

- **Select Ringtone.** Plays a ringtone when a new e-mail arrives. (I prefer to keep my gPhone silent due to the volume of e-mail that I receive.)

- **Vibrate.** Sets your phone to vibrate when a new e-mail arrives.

Figure 5.5
Gmail's general settings allow you to do things like add a signature and receive a status-bar notification when you get new e-mail.

Managing mail

Here's a little trick that saves me a lot of time: Tap and hold a message in the inbox to access mail options without having to open the message. These options are

- **Read.** Allows you to read the message as though you'd tapped it normally. (I know—duh!)

- **Archive.** Moves messages out of your inbox, letting you tidy up your inbox without deleting anything.

- **Mark Read.** Allows you to mark a message as read without having to tap it to do so. This feature is more useful than it sounds and is quicker than loading the whole message.

- **Add Star.** Adds a star next to certain messages or conversations to give them special status. Starred items remain visible when you return to a conversation.

- **Delete.** Removes a message or conversation from Gmail—eventually. *Delete* is actually a misnomer here. When you "delete" an e-mail in Android, it's actually stashed in the Trash folder on the gPhone for 30 days; *then* it's deleted.

> **tip** Deleting can free some of your storage, but with Gmail's free storage, it's best to keep all your e-mails. If you just want to get an e-mail out of your face, I recommend using the Archive option instead.

- **Change Labels.** Changes the label attached to a particular e-mail. Think of labels as being folders with a bonus: You can add more than one label to an e-mail. In your inbox, pressing the Menu key and then tapping View Labels (see the preceding section) allows you to narrow your e-mail view.

- **Report Spam.** Allows you to report a message as spam without opening it. When you do, the offending pork product is removed from your inbox, and you help Google prevent more like it from arriving.

Using the Email application

Not everyone uses Gmail (although you now have an account), so Google includes a more generic Email application on the gPhone that lets you access an unlimited number of POP3 and/or IMAP accounts. Setting up the Email app on the gPhone couldn't be easier, thanks to a convenient wizard that walks you through the process the first time you launch the application (**Figure 5.6**, on the next page).

Figure 5.6

Android's Email wizard makes it easy to set up popular Webmail accounts such as Yahoo! and Hotmail on your gPhone.

note Before you embark on this little journey, you have to provide some information, such as your password, incoming and outgoing e-mail servers, and any special ports. It's best to assemble this information before you start.

Setting up your account

To set up your account by using the Email application's setup wizard, follow these steps:

1. Enter your e-mail address and password (**Figure 5.7**); then tap Next.

   If you enter an address from a popular Webmail service such as Yahoo! or Hotmail, the wizard automatically completes most of the settings for you—a nice feature.

   tip If you're an expert, you can dispense with the wizard and enter your settings in one dense screen by tapping Manual Setup in the bottom-left corner of the first wizard screen.

Figure 5.7
Email's setup wizard first asks for your address and password.

2. In the next screen, tap the button for your e-mail account type (**Figure 5.8**).

   If you're not sure whether your account is POP3 or IMAP, you'll have to ask your Internet service provider (ISP) or the IT staff at your company. If no one is available, try POP3 first. (Even though I prefer IMAP, many providers default to POP3 unless you specifically request an IMAP account.)

Figure 5.8
Would you like the red pill or the blue pill?

3. In the next screen, enter your incoming server settings, including your user name, password, server, port, and security type (**Figure 5.9**, on the next page); then tap Next.

Figure 5.9
*Enter your
incoming server
settings.*

Your user name usually is the first part of your e-mail address, but some ISPs require your complete address as your user name. The IMAP server (or POP3 server) can be anything your ISP desires. Some of the most popular servers simply append *imap.* or *mail.* to the beginning of your domain name, but check with your ISP or the IT folks if you don't know.

> **tip** Instead of waiting on hold with technical support to get your e-mail settings, try checking the incoming and outgoing account information on your desktop computer's e-mail application. You can glean most of the necessary settings here, although your password will be bulleted out. If you can't remember your password, you may have to make that call.

4. Enter your outgoing server settings in the next screen (**Figure 5.10**) and then tap Next.

   The Outgoing Server Settings screen is slightly more complicated than its incoming counterpart due to the Security Type drop-down menu. My ISP requires Secure Sockets Layer (SSL) authentication, so I choose the SSL option from this menu, but your mileage may vary. Check with your e-mail provider for its specific outgoing security type.

note Thanks to the scourge of spam, ISPs have been forced to add security to their outgoing mail servers. The user name and password you enter here usually are the same ones that you use for your e-mail account, but definitely check with your ISP if you're not sure.

Figure 5.10
Now enter your outgoing server settings.

5. Set a few options in the Account Options screen (**Figure 5.11**) and then tap Next:

Figure 5.11
Account options include frequency, default account, and notifications.

- **Frequency of checking e-mail.** This setting is a personal preference. Being a data nut (and somewhat obsessive), I usually choose the shortest checking frequency—in this case, 15 minutes. If Gmail had a setting for 15 *seconds,* I would choose that.

- **Default account.** If this account is the primary account that you want to send e-mail from, check the top check box.

@ • **Notification method.** To have Gmail display an icon in the status bar when a new e-mail arrives, check the bottom check box.

> **note** One really nice aspect of getting e-mail notification in the status bar is that in addition to displaying the e-mail icon, the status bar displays the first several words of the incoming message's subject line.

If all went well, after you tap Next you'll see your inbox (**Figure 5.12**), with your most recent e-mails listed (sender's address, subject line, and date). It's easy to miss, but a green vertical bar on the left edge of the screen indicates an unread message. After you tap a message to read it, the green bar goes away.

Figure 5.12
Wunderbar! *Your e-mail account is set up correctly when you see recent e-mail in the inbox view.*

Reading, replying, and composing

Assuming that you didn't just jump right to this section from the index, you can probably guess how to do most of the things associated with e-mail. Reading, replying to, and composing e-mails are extremely intuitive tasks on the gPhone, and most functions are only a screen tap away.

You handle pretty much everything else by pressing the Menu key and then tapping the desired button (refer to Figure 5.4 earlier in this chapter). Rather than repeat all that information here (this book is a *Pocket Guide*, after all!), I refer you to the "Viewing inbox options" and "Managing mail" sections of the Gmail topic earlier in this chapter.

There you have it. Your e-mail is popping!

Messaging

Whether you're a tween or in your 60s, you've probably figured out by now that text messaging is the new e-mail. In fact, it's the new voice mail and the new everything else these days, at least when it comes to mobile phones.

The extreme convenience of text messaging has undoubtedly contributed to its meteoric rise in popularity over the past decade. It's used by approximately 75 percent of mobile-phone subscribers, translating into 2.4 billion active users and 15 billion messages sent each year. Whew!

Sending messages via Short Message Service (SMS), or just *texting,* is ideal for those times when you want to convey a message that's not long enough for an e-mail or important enough to justify a phone call. It's also handy for times when you don't want to disrupt the recipient with a phone call but can't wait for him to check his e-mail.

Because they're limited to 160 characters (about 25 words, give or take), text messages force you to summarize what you could probably talk about for 20 minutes on the phone or ramble on about for 11 paragraphs in an e-mail. For many people, this very brevity makes texting so powerful—and it doesn't hurt that most phones (including the gPhone) notify you when you have an SMS message via an in-your-face alert.

Like all good technologies, SMS got an upgrade in 2002 to Multimedia Messaging Service (MMS), which allows users to send longer messages and include images, audio, video, and rich text. It's most popular for sending photos from camera-equipped phones.

The Google phone comes with both SMS and MMS in one convenient application called Messaging. In the following sections, I go over some of the features of both types of messaging, so stretch those thumbs; they're about to get a workout.

tip If you get bitten by the texting bug, you need to invest in an unlimited package. It's easy to exceed the number of text messages included in your plan (if you get any, that is), and overages can add up quickly, at 20 cents per outgoing or incoming message. If you have teenage children, just buck up for the unlimited plan, as you'll probably be texting them when dinner is ready.

Short Message Service

The beauty of SMS is its simplicity—no complicated configuration, no difficult settings, and frankly not much to learn. You start using it by launching the Messaging application with a simple tap. When the application loads, you see the Messaging inbox, displaying the messages you've received in reverse chronological order (**Figure 5.13**). Like the Gmail and Email applications, which I cover earlier in this chapter, Messaging displays a green vertical bar on the left edge of unread messages.

Figure 5.13
The Messaging inbox is a lot like your computer's e-mail inbox, with the newest messages appearing at the top.

The first 35 characters of received messages are visible in the inbox view, along with the sender, time, and date. If the sender is in your contact list (see Chapter 3 for more on contacts), you'll see her proper name displayed; if not, you see just her mobile-phone number. Messages sent from your carrier (such as the one from 456 in Figure 5.13) often display partial numbers and don't accept replies. Fortunately, carriers usually don't charge for these messages.

The quickest way to compose a message is to tap the first line in the Messaging inbox, labeled New Message. Another way is to press the Menu key, tap the Compose button, enter a contact's name (or phone number) in the To field, write a message, and then tap Send.

When you receive a text or multimedia message, a notification icon in the status bar tells you so. Slide the status bar down and tap the message to go directly to the Messaging app's detail view (**Figure 5.14**), where you can view the entire conversation (if any) and reply to the sender. Tapping any message in the inbox also takes you to detail view.

Figure 5.14
The Messaging app's detail view allows you to see the entire thread of an SMS/MMS conversation, similar to an instant-message conversation.

To set SMS options, press the Menu key and then tap the Settings button. The SMS Settings screen (**Figure 5.15**, on the next page) contains several options that are pretty self-explanatory, thanks to the help text below each option.

Figure 5.15

The SMS Settings screen is one of the longest on the gPhone and includes useful options such as Delivery Reports.

tip The coolest feature of SMS and MMS messages is the Delivery Reports option. When you enable this option, the gPhone sends you a message to confirm that your outgoing message reached its destination—similar to a return receipt from the post office. Unfortunately, this feature isn't a perfect science, so don't rely on it to be 100 accurate.

Multimedia Messaging Service

Multimedia Messaging Service (MMS) is the next generation of SMS. In addition to sending a vanilla text message, you can attach images, audio, video, and rich text, so comparing MMS with SMS is like comparing a banana split with a vanilla cone. A better analogy would be comparing SMS and MMS with plain text and HTML e-mails.

Although MMS is super-useful for sending photos from camera-equipped phones (like most Google phones), it can also be annoying when you go

off the deep end and send a birthday card that includes an animated
singing frog. As with most things in life, discretion is the better part of
valor when it comes to MMS.

To send an MMS, tap New Message at the top of the Messaging inbox
(refer to Figure 5.13 earlier in this chapter), or tap Menu > Compose. Add
a recipient and some text; then tap Menu > Attach. The resulting screen
(**Figure 5.16**) allows you to attach pictures, audio, or even a slideshow.

Figure 5.16
*You can attach
several types of
media to MMS
messages, which
makes MMS more
powerful than
simple SMS.*

note Before going hog-wild with all kinds of fancy media attachments,
make sure that your recipient can accept MMS messages. If he can't,
he'll get a strange message asking him to log into a Web page to retrieve it. If
you're not certain that your recipient has an MMS-capable phone, send an SMS
message instead.

Web Browsing

By this point in the book, I hope that I don't have to explain the power of
the Web. Because you've invested in a Google phone (or are considering
investing in one), you're probably a pretty Web-savvy person. Because
my cats are fairly proficient at using the Web (maybe *that's* where those

preapproved credit-card offers are coming from!), I'd like to assume that you are too. (Check that—my editor told me not to assume anything in this book.)

That said, the World Wide Web gives you access to more information than kings and rulers of land had as little as 100 years ago. The Web is a much faster way to get information, too. Rather than having to dispatch a legion of serfs across land and sea to gather information, you can simply type a few keywords in Google, and boom!—thousands of results (or even millions) are at your disposal. Results are returned in milliseconds, rather than days/weeks/months or even years. What did we do before Google?

In all seriousness, the importance, utility, and convenience of the Web are irrefutable. The Web allows you to research a book (ahem!); get prices, reviews, and dealer costs for just about anything; perform online banking; attend meetings; and buy and sell all kinds of items. On the gPhone, you start by tapping the Browser icon.

Mobile browsers

Although expectations can be high, it's important to understand that mobile Web browsers aren't perfect. You're limited to a small screen and keyboard, and have less memory and storage. Another important limitation of the gPhone is that the browser can't display Adobe Flash content. Otherwise, mobile-phone browsers operate pretty much like the browsers on desktop computers. You can zoom in, zoom out, and move inside a Web page.

Odds are that you've used a browser before (yes?), so I won't go into detail on the basics of a Web address and the like. Instead, I'll focus on how a mobile browser differs from a desktop Web browser.

First, though, some technical background is in order. Google uses WebKit as its browser in Android. (This application framework also powers Apple's Safari and Nokia's S60 browser.) Although WebKit does an adequate job of rendering complex Web pages, it can be slow at times. Like all good technologies, it will get better over time.

The gPhone browser

To use the gPhone's Web browser, simply tap the aptly named Browser application. The browser displays a cached version of the last page you were browsing. To navigate to a Web page, press the Menu key; tap the Go to URL button at the bottom of the screen (**Figure 5.17**); enter the Web address that you want to visit; and tap Go.

Figure 5.17
The Google phone's Web browser, with Menu-key options displayed.

tip   If you're not sure of the Web address, you can enter a search term in the address field (such as *Google Phone Pocket Guide*), and you'll get search results from Google. You can also tap the Search button to do the same thing.

You have several ways to navigate a Web page, but I find the most convenient to be simply dragging a finger around on the touchscreen. You can also use the trackball to scroll around on a page. When you're browsing a page that's too large for the gPhone's screen, you can slide the screen up (in the case of the G1) to use the wider landscape format. I find it a little easier to read long Web pages in landscape mode, but you should experiment with both portrait and landscape modes to see which works better for you.

If you're browsing a Web page that's not optimized for the small screen, tapping anywhere on the screen reveals two small magnifying-glass icons at the bottom of the screen (**Figure 5.18**). As you've probably guessed, you tap the plus (+) and minus (–) icons to zoom in and out of a Web page, respectively. Tapping the four-headed-arrow icon (called the *zoom box*) in the bottom-right corner shrinks large Web pages to fit on one screen and lets you drag your finger across the screen to the part of the page you want to see. Although the zoom box is a little awkward to manipulate at first, you'll find yourself using this feature a lot.

Figure 5.18
Zoom controls and a zoom box appear at the bottom of the screen when you tap a large Web page.

Tap to shrink and drag the page

Tap to zoom in

Tap to zoom out

Shopping on the Run

When you're using the browser to search Google, you see a new icon to the right of the Search button—an icon that looks like a miniature bar code (**Figure 5.19**). If you tap it, you can download a free Android application called Barcode Scanner, which lets you use the gPhone's camera to scan bar codes and then look up product information such as prices and reviews.

Figure 5.19
Bar-code searching from the gPhone gives e-commerce a new level of power.

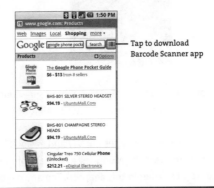

Tap to download Barcode Scanner app

Bookmarks, windows, and settings

The Android Web browser functions just like a desktop browser, right down to the bookmarks. Rather than tap out the same Web address over and over, create a bookmark, which is much faster. To bookmark the page that you're viewing, tap Menu > More > Bookmark Page.

To navigate to a page that you've already bookmarked, press the Menu key; then tap the Bookmarks button (refer to Figure 5.17 earlier in this chapter). The browser displays your bookmarks in reverse chronological order, including each bookmark's name and URL (**Figure 5.20**, on the next page).

To go to a bookmark, you can tap it or select it with the trackball and then click the trackball.

Figure 5.20
The browser's Bookmarks screen. Just tap and go.

If you're a power browser, having several browser windows open at the same time is convenient. Unfortunately, the gPhone's screen isn't large enough for browser tabs. Instead, a built-in Window feature allows you to navigate up to four Web pages quickly and easily (**Figure 5.21**). To access this feature, press the Menu key and then tap the Window button (refer to Figure 5.17 earlier in this chapter). Tap any page that you see in the Current Windows screen to go to that page, or tap the New Window option in the top-left corner to go to a different page.

Figure 5.21
Android's Window feature is like tabbed browsing for the small screen.

Settings Galore

If you're into tweaking settings, you'll be in heaven when you tap Menu > More > Settings in the Android browser. The resulting settings screen is easily the longest I've seen in any Android application (four scrolls!) and rivals the settings screen in most desktop browsers.

The first section covers the page-content settings and allows you to set up the text size and things like pop-up blocking and loading images. For the most part, I leave these settings alone.

The second section focuses on privacy settings and allows you to clear the cache, history, and cookies. The Remember Form Data option is extremely helpful, because it saves you from having to enter the same information (such as your user name and password) on pages that you visit frequently. The Security section allows you to remember and clear passwords. (Saving form data isn't recommended for sensitive sites such as banking and e-commerce, because if you lose your phone, the person who finds it can look through your history and bookmarks, as well as log into your accounts. Never save logins for sensitive sites on your gPhone.)

The advanced section allows you to enable and customize Google Gears. This app allows you to extend the browser's functionality by saving pages for offline viewing, which is eminently useful at times when you may be without Internet connectivity, such as when you're on a commercial flight. Gears allows you to keep working when most people are forced to play solitaire.

Rounding out the browser's menu options are a Refresh button, which reloads the page that you're viewing (which can be helpful when tickets for Phish at Red Rocks are about to go on sale); and a More button, which reveals navigation options and functions for sharing, bookmarking, and viewing a page's information (**Figure 5.22**).

Figure 5.22
More browser options.

6

Fun with Multimedia

The past several chapters are rather utilitarian, focusing on tools like e-mail, messaging, and contacts. Now it's time to let your hair down a little and have some fun with the Google phone. In this chapter, I run down all the multimedia options that are available on the G1, including pictures, music, and movies. Let's have some fun, shall we?

note Numerous third-party applications that play (and record) multimedia are available from the Android Market. This chapter focuses on the applications that are included with the phone; I cover third-party applications and the Market in Chapter 7.

Camera

One of the greatest features of most modern smartphones is the built-in camera. No, it's not going to win any competitions for quality; neither is it going to replace your trusty digital camera. You always have it with you, though, and it's simple to snap and send a picture with it. It's great for those "playing at the park" e-mails to Nanny and for those times when you want to get your significant other's opinion on a piece of furniture or clothing.

The Google phone ships with two primary applications that you'll use for photographs: Camera and Pictures.

Shooting pictures

To take a picture on the gPhone, simply tap the Camera icon in the application drawer. You're ready to shoot as soon as the screen turns into a live viewfinder (**Figure 6.1**). Compose your photo on the gPhone's screen, and press the shutter-release button located on the bottom-right side of the gPhone. (Your Google phone's shutter-release button may be in a different location, depending on which model you have.)

Figure 6.1

The gPhone's screen turns into a viewfinder when you're in shooting mode.

tip   Keep your phone as still as possible when you're shooting pictures. A pretty significant lag occurs between the time when you press the shutter-release button and the time when the gPhone actually records the photo, making it difficult to take pictures of kids and pets. For best results, try to keep your hands—and your subjects—still for a full second after you press the button.

After the picture is taken, you'll see a row of buttons along the bottom of the screen (**Figure 6.2**).

Figure 6.2
After you snap a photo, you see this menu.

The menu buttons work this way:

- **Save.** Unlike some camera phones, the gPhone doesn't save your picture automatically. You have to tap the Save button.

- **Set As.** After shooting, you can tap the Set As button to use the photo as a contact icon, which will be displayed onscreen when that contact calls you, or as wallpaper for your gPhone's home screen. (See Chapter 3 for more info on contacts.)

- **Share.** The Share button allows you to send a photo to a friend immediately via the phone's Email, Gmail, or Messaging application.

    note   Some third-party applications, such as I Tweet!, modify this menu so that you can share photos from the Camera application directly to Twitter. (I cover third-party applications in Chapter 7.)

- **Delete.** Use the Delete option to trash pictures that are blurry or poorly composed.

Changing camera settings

While you're using the camera, press the Menu key to access options that let you jump over to the Pictures application (more on it in the following section) or change settings (**Figure 6.3**).

Figure 6.3
Pressing the Menu key gives you access to Pictures and Settings options.

When you tap the Settings button, you see two options:

- **Store Location in Pictures.** Uses the gPhone's Global Positioning System (GPS) chip to record your location in the picture data— a process called *geotagging*. This feature is turned off by default to save battery power.

- **Prompt After Capture.** Displays the menu shown in Figure 6.2 earlier in this chapter after you press the shutter-release button. This option is enabled by default; disable it for faster picture-taking.

Taking pictures with your gPhone's camera is definitely an art, and getting it right takes a little practice. If you're patient and have a steady hand, however, the output from the gPhone's camera can be quite acceptable.

Pictures

Whereas the Camera application captures photos, its partner application, Pictures, manages photos. Launch Pictures from the application drawer, and you'll see thumbnail images of 12 pictures at a time (**Figure 6.4**) in the image browser. Flick your finger up, down, and across the screen to scroll to the other pictures in your library.

Figure 6.4
When you launch Pictures, you see thumbnails of all your saved photos in the image browser.

Viewing pictures

To see a picture in full-screen mode, just tap its thumbnail in the image browser. When you're in full-screen mode, tapping anywhere on the screen gives you several image options (**Figure 6.5**), including Forward and Backward arrows and the same Zoom In (+) and Zoom Out (–) icons that the Browser application uses (see Chapter 5).

Figure 6.5
If you tap a picture in full-screen mode, you see navigation arrows and zoom icons (which you can tap to make the minnow you caught look much bigger).

Tap the right arrow to advance to the next image or the left arrow to go back to the preceding image. The zoom icons allow you to zoom into and out of an image. Don't zoom too far, though; the gPhone's 3.2-megapixel camera is limited.

Changing picture settings

After you've built up a library of pictures (if you're like me, this won't take long), you can really have some fun with them. It's not much fun to keep all your photos bottled up in your gPhone, so why not share them with friends in the moment? You don't need to wait to get home from a trip to share your photos; send a photo of yourself at the beach *from* the beach.

When you're in full-screen mode, press the Menu key to reveal a list of choices (**Figure 6.6**):

- **Slideshow.** Displays your photos as a slideshow, advancing the photos automatically with a dissolve effect between pictures—great for the plane ride home.

- **Share.** Allows you to send a picture to a friend via the gPhone's Email, Gmail, or Messaging app, just like the Share button in the Camera application.

- **Rotate.** Turns your photo left or right in 90-degree increments.

- **Flip Orientation.** Allows you to flip the orientation of the Pictures *application*, not of the photo itself. By default, Pictures uses portrait orientation, but if you find yourself taking most of your photos in landscape orientation, by all means give this button a tap.

- **Delete.** Banishes the current photo to the trash.

Figure 6.6
The Pictures menu options allow you to share, flip, and delete photos, among other things.

But wait! I can almost hear you saying, "There's one more button in Figure 6.6!" You're correct. The last button in the Pictures menu is More, which reveals another menu that offers even more options (**Figure 6.7**).

Figure 6.7
The infamous More button reveals yet another menu.

These options are

- **Crop.** Lets you crop an image down to the good part easily by dragging an onscreen bounding box with your finger.

- **Set As.** Allows you to set a picture as a contact icon or as your phone's wallpaper. This feature works just like the Set As option in the Camera application (see "Shooting pictures" earlier in this chapter).

- **Details.** Shows the details of a photo, including its file name, size, and resolution, and the date it was taken.

- **Settings.** Opens the General Settings screen (**Figure 6.8**). This screen is quite extensive, including options for changing the display size and sort order of pictures. You can also set an option to have the gPhone ask you to confirm before deleting pictures. More useful are the slideshow settings, which allow you to change the slideshow interval (unfortunately, your choices are limited to 2, 3, or 4 seconds) and the transition effect. Finally, you can set options to repeat the slideshow and to shuffle the pictures instead of playing them in the order in which they were taken.

Figure 6.8
*Tapping Menu >
More > Settings
brings up
the Pictures
application's
General Settings
screen.*

Music

Now that you're an expert at taking and managing pictures with your Google phone, it's time to relax with some music. In addition to being a capable phone and camera, the gPhone makes a great jukebox.

Before you begin jamming on your gPhone, though, you need to transfer some music to it. All music on your phone is stored on a MicroSDHC

(Micro Secure Digital High Capacity) card inserted into your phone's expansion-card slot. The Music application won't run unless this card is installed (see Chapter 2).

tip Although the 1 GB card included with your Google phone is capable, you'll fill it fast. I recommend that you splurge on an 8 GB or 16 GB card; these cards aren't too expensive.

Android's Music application supports the following audio file formats:

- AAC (.3gp, .mp4, .m4a)
- MP3 (.mp3)
- MIDI (.mid and others)
- Ogg Vorbis (.ogg)
- PCM/WAVE (.wav)

Transferring music

To transfer music to the MicroSDHC card in your Google phone, follow these steps:

1. Make sure that a MicroSDHC card is inserted into the phone's expansion-card slot (see Chapter 2).

2. Enable USB storage mode by tapping Settings > SD Card & Phone Storage > Use for USB Storage.

3. Connect the gPhone to your computer with the included USB cable.

4. Wait for the MicroSDHC card to mount on the Desktop (Mac OS X) or in the Removable Disk folder (Windows).

5. Create a folder on the MicroSDHC card called Music.

6. Drag and drop (or copy and paste) music files from your computer to the Music folder that you just created.

7. Eject the card from your computer.

8. Launch the Music application.

tip Another way to transfer music to the gPhone is to insert the MicroSDHC card into an SD card carrier and then insert the carrier into a card reader connected to your computer. At that point, you can copy the files to the card.

Playing music

When you launch the Music application by tapping its icon in the application drawer, you see the main interface (**Figure 6.9**), which is neatly divided into four logical areas that narrow your music down to artists, albums, songs, and playlists. If you can't find what you're looking for, press the Menu key and tap Search. Alternatively, if you're not in the mood to think, tap Party Shuffle for a randomly selected playlist.

Figure 6.9
The Music application is divided into four logical areas, shown here with the Menu-key options at the bottom.

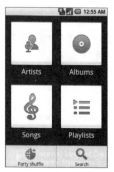

Artists view

Artists view (**Figure 6.10**) displays all the music on your memory card sorted by artist. Flick up and down (or use the trackball) to scroll. (Oh, and about the music selection in the figure—I'm a product of the '80s. What can I say?) Tap any artist to drill down to all the songs by that artist; tap a song to start playing it.

Figure 6.10
The Music application's Artists view, shown here with OMD expanded.

When you start playing a song, you see the detail view (**Figure 6.11**), which provides some basic information about the song. Below the album artwork are the artist, album, and song name.

Figure 6.11
Detail view gives you lots of information and options.

To the right are three buttons to tap for more songs by this artist, shuffle mode, and repeat mode. At the bottom of the screen, you find standard rewind, play, and fast-forward controls, as well as a music timeline that tells you where you are in the song, both visually and numerically.

Albums view

Albums view, as you've probably guessed, displays your music sorted by album (**Figure 6.12**). This view is helpful when you have a lot of complete albums but can get kind of long when you have a mishmosh of music or a bunch of music from one particular genre. (I have a lot of '80s music loaded on my gPhone, so Albums view is very long.) Albums view displays the album artwork (assuming that you have it), album name, artist, and number of songs from that album that you have loaded on your memory card.

Figure 6.12
Albums view conveniently displays album artwork inline.

Songs view

Songs view (**Figure 6.13**) is also pretty self-explanatory, displaying every song loaded on your memory card. Below each song name are the album name and the artist; to the right is the song's running time. Simply tap

any song to play it, or flick your finger up and down on the screen until
you find something that you like.

Figure 6.13
*Songs view
displays every
song on your
memory card.
Beware—this list
can get long.*

> **tip** One of my favorite things to do in Songs view is flick-shuffle, which
> involves giving the song list a good flick and then randomly tapping
> the screen to stop at a song. Think of this technique as being like spinning that
> big wheel in the Showcase Showdown on "The Price Is Right," except that you
> don't have to wait for the wheel to stop.

Playlists view

The Google phone supports .m3u playlists, which it reads from the
MicroSDHC card.

> **note** An .m3u file is a text file that contains the location of media files. Your
> music-player software reads the .m3u file to see what order to play the
> media files in.

If you want to use playlists, create a Playlists folder inside the Music
folder on your memory card and copy your .m3u files to it. After you
do, your playlists will show up when you tap the Playlists button in the
Music screen (refer to Figure 6.9).

More Than Music

You can also use music and audio files from your computer as alarms, notifications, and ringtones on the gPhone. Simply create folders on the root level of the MicroSDHC card named Alarms, Notifications, and Ringtones; then copy the appropriate files to the correct folder. The next time you set an alarm, notification, or ringtone, you'll see your music files as choices. Cool!

YouTube

As I mention in Chapter 1, Google acquired YouTube in 2006 for $1.65 billion, so if you bet that Google would include a YouTube player on the gPhone, you'd be correct!

YouTube for Android is more than just a simple video player. In fact, it includes several features that are available on YouTube.com, including a huge catalog of keyword-searchable videos and browsing by most popular, most viewed, top rated, most recent, and most discussed videos.

When you tap the YouTube icon to launch the YouTube application, you see featured videos across the top of the screen; below are a thumbnail image of the selected video and its running time, star rating, title, and description (**Figure 6.14**). Flick your finger left and right across the videos at the top of the screen to scroll through them. Below the featured videos are subsections listing the most popular, most viewed, top rated, most recent, and most discussed videos on YouTube. These lists are a great way to keep yourself entertained on a long trip without having to search for video (provided that you have an Internet connection).

Figure 6.14
*The main
YouTube interface
shows featured
videos and
shortcuts to the
most popular
videos from the
video sharing site.*

> **note** YouTube on Android is limited to videos encoded in H.264/MPEG-4.
> This means that only videos encoded in H.264 will play on the Google
> phone; videos encoded in Adobe Flash are *not* supported.

Tapping the Menu key reveals four options (**Figure 6.15**):

Figure 6.15
*YouTube's Menu-
key options
include Search
and Categories.*

- **Search.** Allows you to search for videos by entering example text (such
  as *"I'm on a Boat"*).
- **Favorites.** Displays videos that you tag as favorites on the gPhone.

- **Categories.** Displays a list of more than 50 categories of videos, including People & Blogs, Science & Technology, and Pets & Animals.

- **Settings.** Provides a single option: Clear Search History.

note At this writing, YouTube for Android doesn't allow you to log into your account at YouTube.com. Think of the gPhone as being an island in this case, with your favorites on the phone being separate from your favorites on YouTube.com. This arrangement may change in the future, but for now, that's the way it is.

So there you have it. The Google phone just got a little more fun, thanks to a few of its built-in applications. Take some time to learn the lighter side of Android. It can be great to share your pictures, unwind to some tunes, and get a quick laugh courtesy of a video on YouTube.

Now that I've covered most of the included applications on Android, it's time to cast a wider net. In Chapter 7, I give you an overview of the Android Market, where you can choose among thousands of applications to download and review some of the best ones available from this wonderful resource.

7

Android Market

The most powerful and fun application on the Google phone is the Android Market. It's powerful because the Market allows you to browse and download hundreds of free and paid applications directly to your gPhone, usually in less than a minute. It's fun because there's literally no limit to the types of applications that you can find for the gPhone at the Android Market. There's something for everyone.

Part of the strength of the Market is its catalog of applications. Although it's not quite as deep as some of the other players out there (ahem, Apple!), this online store is a high-quality, easy-to-use source of tons of useful apps.

In this chapter, I take a closer look at how to use the Android Market and highlight some of the best applications that I've found there. First, though, a short history lesson is in order.

History and Background

The first Google phone—the T-Mobile G1—was released on October 22, 2008, to much fanfare. Although the G1 included lots of useful applications such as Browser, Contacts, and Calendar, its Market application was kind of bare. The entire Market consisted of a couple of basic games and hokey alarm clocks, and not much else.

That's because when Android first shipped, Google hadn't yet implemented its pay-to-download infrastructure, so all the software in the Market was free. Without the potential for profit, developers were hesitant to invest their time writing applications for the gPhone—and who could blame them?—so the offerings initially available for download were mediocre at best.

All that changed in February 2009, when paid applications were made available to Android users in the United States. Since then, Android Market has matured into an enticing platform for developers to write for, as well as a treasure chest of goodies for owners of Google phones.

How to Use It

The Market application comes preinstalled on all Android-powered phones. To launch it, simply tap the Market icon—the one with the friendly robot on a shopping bag. Like most applications for Android, Market has a drop-dead-simple interface. When you launch the app, you're greeted by a home screen (**Figure 7.1**) that features five primary areas:

Figure 7.1
The Android Market's home screen has five simple options.

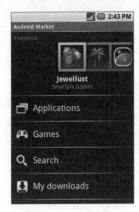

- **Featured.** Across the top of the Market screen are its featured apps. The colorful icons are kind of hard to miss. Google constantly updates the Featured section of the Market, so it's a good idea to check periodically to see what's new.

  Slide your finger left and right across the featured-app icons to scroll through them. Tap an icon to display the detail view for that application (**Figure 7.2**).

Figure 7.2
Tapping the icon for any application takes you to the detail view, where you can read a description of the app and user comments.

- **Applications.** This area is a general catch-all for all applications. Tapping it reveals a list of categories, such as Communication, Finance, and Reference. Tapping a category produces a list of all the applications in that category, sorted by either popularity or date.

- **Games.** This area of the Market is for the gamer in you. Tap it to drill down to applications that developers have classified as games, listed in categories such as Arcade & Action, Brain & Puzzle, Cards & Casino, and Casual. At this writing, the most popular games in the Market include Pac-Man, Solitaire, and Labyrinth Lite.

- **Search.** I spend most of my time in the Market using its search feature. To use it, simply tap Search and then type a few keywords in the search field. A search for *golf* in May 2009 produced 21 results, including applications for keeping score and tracking your exact position on the course via satellite—not to mention golf jokes.

- **My Downloads.** This area is where you can see all the applications that you've downloaded to date. It's a convenient way to see whether any app updates are pending for your gPhone and to be reminded of past downloads that you may have forgotten about. I cover this feature in more detail in "Updating Market Apps" later in this chapter.

Caveats of Buying

When you've found an application that you like, keep a few things in mind before tapping the Buy button:

- **Returns.** Android Market accepts returns within 24 hours of purchase. The clock starts ticking when you download the app, not when you install it, so you should try to use an app immediately after installing it.

- **Reinstallations.** Android Market allows you to reinstall purchased apps an unlimited number of times at no charge. This feature can come in handy if a download gets interrupted or corrupted (although I've never known that to happen), your gPhone runs out of storage space, or a reset is necessary.

- **Updates.** Although Google policy states that you should obtain application upgrades directly from the developers, your gPhone will notify you with a status-bar icon (**Figure 7.3**) when updates are released to address bugs or complaints or to add features.

Figure 7.3
A status-bar icon notifies you when updates are available for apps you've downloaded from the Android Market.

Updates icon

note Google makes it clear that it bears no responsibility for billing disputes that result from the Android Market. If you have any problems with an app, your best recourse is to request a refund within 24 hours. If you have a problem after that, you have to take it up with the developer—or with your credit card company.

Updating Market Apps

When a developer releases an update for a Market application you've downloaded, your phone displays a notification icon in the status bar, showing a white shopping bag with the Android icon on it (refer to Figure 7.3 in the preceding section). Swipe your finger down over the status bar to reveal the details on any app updates that are available (**Figure 7.4**, on the next page). Then simply tap Updates Available and follow the prompts to install the updates.

Figure 7.4
The Android Market Notifications screen reveals any updates that are available for downloaded apps.

The other way to check for updates of applications that you've downloaded is to launch Market and tap the last option in the Market's home screen: My Downloads (refer to Figure 7.1 earlier in this chapter). Applications that have updates pending are displayed at the top of the My Downloads screen (**Figure 7.5**); tap each update in turn to install the updates individually.

Figure 7.5
The My Downloads section of the Android Market home screen shows any available application updates.

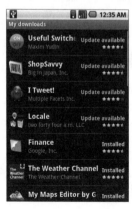

note Unfortunately, the Market doesn't give you an easy way to update all your applications at the same time. Perhaps we'll see this feature added in a future update of the Market application?

Application Spotlight

Following are some of the most interesting applications that I've discovered in my travels around the Android Market. Some are free, and some are paid (as noted); feel free to try all of them out.

ShopSavvy

Price: Free
Developer: Big in Japan, Inc. (www.biggu.com)
Shop Savvy (**Figure 7.6**) won the 2008 Android Developer Challenge. Think of it as your personal shopping assistant. It uses the camera in your phone to scan the bar code on any product and then finds the best prices on the Internet and at nearby local stores.

Figure 7.6
ShopSavvy allows you to compare prices with your gPhone.

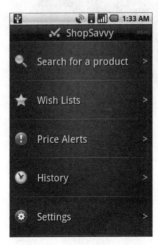

TuneWiki

Price: Free

Developer: TuneWiki (www.TuneWiki.com)

TuneWiki (**Figure 7.7**) bills itself as being a social media player. In addition to being an advanced player, it features synchronized lyrics for audio or video, translation, music maps, and a social network. TuneWiki uses patented technology that allows you to listen to songs while watching the lyrics scroll by.

Figure 7.7
TuneWiki offers more than just music. In addition to playing music and videos, it scrolls the lyrics across the bottom of the screen.

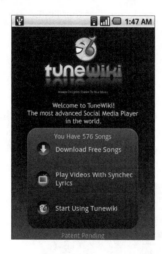

I Tweet!

Price: $2.99

Developer: Multiple Facets, Inc. (www.multiplefacets.com/twitterblog)

Bitten by the Twitter bug? If you are, the best Twitter client for Android is I Tweet! (**Figure 7.8**). It allows you to post tweets and direct messages with your location and photos, retweet, view profiles, and search by keyword and even location. If you're a Twitterer, this app is definitely the one to get; if you're not, consider yourself lucky that you haven't gotten hooked on this addictive social networking service. Hey, there's always golf instead.

Figure 7.8

The main screen of I Tweet! has a tabbed interface to ease navigation.

The Weather Channel

Price: Free

Developer: The Weather Channel Mobile (www.weather.com/mobile)

One of the most useful aspects of the gPhone is being able to check the weather on a moment's notice from wherever you are. It's super-convenient to know what the weather will be before you have to travel or even just before you leave for your morning commute. The Weather Channel's mobile app (**Figure 7.9**) is the best of the lot. It allows you to use your gPhone to access severe-weather warnings, forecasts, and radar maps for your city and thousands of other cities worldwide.

Figure 7.9
The Weather Channel's Android application has a convenient ten-day view.

Locale

Price: Free

Developer: two forty four a.m. (www.twofortyfouram.com)

Locale (**Figure 7.10**) won the grand prize in the 2008 Android Developer Challenge (take *that*, ShopSavvy!) for turning location management into an art form. Locale dynamically manages all of your Google phone's settings based on conditions such as location and time. You can use it, for example, to set up a condition that turns off 3G and switches to your home Wi-Fi network as soon as the phone is in range. You can even set things so that designated VIP callers always ring through, no matter how you've set the phone's ringer volume.

Figure 7.10

Locale takes settings management to the extreme, allowing you to change your phone settings based on location or time.

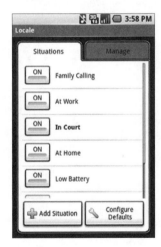

That's a Wrap

So there you have it, folks! You've had a good look at everything from unboxing your gPhone to configuring it to installing applications on it.

I hope that you enjoyed reading this book as much as I enjoyed writing it. More important, I hope that this book helps you squeeze a little extra performance and utility out of what promises to be the Swiss Army knife of smartphones: the Google phone.

Index